to

from

The first place I went after losing our baby to miscarriage was the bookstore. I stared at the shelves looking for words of comfort and hope, longing to find an author who would also feel like a friend putting her arm around my shoulder. I wish Sarah's book had been there then, and I'm so grateful it will be there for other women like me now.

—Holley Gerth, *best-selling author of* You're Already Amazing, *holleygerth.com*

Our culture programs us to feel as though motherhood should be all sunshine and roses—breakfasts in bed made by beaming, freshly-bathed children. We learn to think that a woman cannot fulfill her God-given destiny unless she nurtures the lives God enabled her to bear. And yet, when one of those lives is lost, or when life never begins, the world suddenly goes quiet, leaving these women alone and suffering. Here's the key, though: When we offer our hurts to God, He will bring healing. He is the salve that soothes even the deepest wounds. Through Sarah's words in *Loved Baby*, you will realize that you're not called to forget but to welcome God into your pain. You can remember and honor and grieve and be made whole again. With God, even this is possible. Step into these pages like you're walking into God's comforting embrace, because that's exactly what this book has to offer.

—Kelly O'Dell Stanley, *author of* Praying Upside Down *and* Designed to Pray, *kellyostanley.com*

This book is the one I wish I'd had when I lost my first son the day after he was born sleeping and my third son when I was fifteen-weeks pregnant. For my aching, searching heart to have God's truths and promises put together so compassionately and with such honesty would have been a gift, and one I now will graciously share with others who have to walk this life-changing path. God's goodness and comfort flow freely from Sarah's heart and will bring healing and redemption to so many.

—Lori Mullin Ennis, *editor of* Still Standing Magazine

"Your numbers have dropped," the nurse said. "Let us know if the bleeding starts filling a pad every hour. I'm sorry." And with that, I learned I was about to have my first miscarriage and second pregnancy loss. A few days later, without bleeding or cramping in sight, I took my husband to Barnes & Noble. I wanted to find something—anything—I could read that would tell me what to expect. The books I found (which weren't much) focused on family planning, or, get this, how *not* to have a miscarriage. Seriously? Women who miscarry needed help, and I found nothing that offered it. In the meantime, our story kept going through three more losses and our time with Z and finally our rainbow pregnancy with Ellie. Thank goodness some of our friends have been in the trenches and are ready to share their hearts and encouragement to women who need a worthwhile resource. Sarah Philpott is one of my friends in the baby loss community. Her book *Loved Baby* is a devotional and journal for baby loss moms. You will want to get this book in your hands!

—*Rachel Lewis, writer, foster mom, adoptive mom,*
biological mom, thelewisnote.com

I have known Sarah Philpott since the moment she was born. As the doctor who delivered her into this world in 1982, I experienced the joy that comes with new life. I have known her family for over fifty years. In fact, I delivered for her mother when she gave birth to her child born still. I have marveled at Sarah's growth into a talented, deeply Christian wife, mother, and community servant. She is a dynamic, persistent, and dedicated young woman. Her career has consisted of writing many professional publications. Her dedication to intense research and careful analysis, combined with her innate skills interviewing and bonding with other women who have had similar outcomes, has resulted in this inspiring narrative, *Loved Baby*. She informs the reader about the trials and struggles mothers and fathers face in their post-loss journeys. She gives hope to those who think they will never conceive again or be successful at giving birth following the loss of a child. As the readers of this beautiful testimony will find out, Sarah has succeeded in giving others, even in the darkest times of their grief, the courage to face challenges and to return to a life of normalcy. She has walked with God on her path and knows that, through all things, if our faith is strong and the support of our beloved family and friends is present, we can overcome the adversities associated with this devastating occurrence. It is a distinct honor and pleasure to recommend Sarah's heart-felt thoughts to those who have endured pregnancy loss and those who try to help and support their loved ones. *Loved Baby* will fill you with healing, hope, and God's love.

—*Shelley F. Griffith, MD*

"They instinctively knew to show me quiet love" is only one example of the exquisite healing words Sarah Philpott uses to help those of us grieving after a pregnancy loss. Her remarkable insights, coupled with her enormous compassion, give us the guidance and strength we need to walk through this devastating journey and know we are not alone. If you have ever loved someone who has suffered through a pregnancy loss, *Loved Baby* may well be the answer to a prayer. I am grateful for Sarah's ability to impart her wisdom and spirituality, hope and grace for all of those who will benefit the most. And bless the beautiful babies in heaven who will live on in our souls forever.

—Lisa Leshaw, MS, CMHC mental health professional

Christian women who have known the unfathomable pain of pregnancy loss at any stage need this devotional. The writer Sarah Philpott is with you on your journey, and through her transparency regarding her own loss, recovery, and faith walk, she offers guidance on healing for mothers post-loss.

—Autumn L. Carusillo, PHD, LCSW

The death of a baby is one of the worst and most traumatic experiences of a parent's life. The grief that follows is all-consuming and often isolating. Sarah Philpott has created a way for parents to process their own grief journey while being reassured they are not alone. *Loved Baby* is a beautiful resource for bereaved parents in their darkest days.

—Lindsey J. Wimmer, CPNP, CPLC,
executive director of Star Legacy Foundation

Loved Baby left me spellbound. I cried and rejoiced at the same time at the healing power that God can bring.

—Jenn Hand, author of 31 Days of Coming Alive
and director of Coming Alive Ministries

I wish I'd had this book to read days after my loss instead of using "Dr. Google" and the like for information on miscarriage.

—Emily Aziz, CPA

In this book, you will feel like Sarah is speaking directly to you as a gentle friend and a loving sister. She truly understands the pain of loss and has a beautiful way with comforting words and practical advice. I love that she pairs godly encouragement with factual information about child loss to help address all parts of grieving: the intellectual, spiritual, physical, and emotional. If I had *Loved Baby* as a resource during the darkest stages of my miscarriage, I certainly would not have felt so alone. The Loved Baby ministry was instrumental in my healing, and I have faith that this book will be instrumental in yours.

—Rosemary Ferrera, mother, former Miss Virginia,
& Christian blogger, SoulStrongFitness.com

Loved Baby is the book I wish I had after my first loss. Sarah Philpott is like a loving sister who has been there, guiding us through. I love the easy-to-apply soul work sections. I cried through most of the book. I would say that even after months and months of grief counseling, reading almost every book out there about pregnancy loss and how to cope, and being in a support group, *Loved Baby* is what brought me the rest of the way. I can't even find the best words to tell you how extremely helpful this is going to be for so many women.

—Jessica Knipprath, mother

I feel like this book was instrumental in my healing from my miscarriages, almost seven years since my last one.

—Jenny Tilley, RN

Loved Baby deals with a topic so dear to my heart because of my experience with three years of infertility and the loss I experienced with my first two babies. I would have given anything to have someone walk me through that season with spiritual insight as well as personal experience. This is why I am thrilled about my friend, Sarah Philpott's new book. Whether you are still grieving or not, you can trust her with your heart.

—Jennifer Watson, author, pastor,
and writer, jenniferreneewatson.com

loved baby

31 DEVOTIONS
Helping You
Grieve and Cherish Your Child
after Pregnancy Loss

Sarah Philpott

BroadStreet Publishing® Group, LLC
Savage, Minnesota, USA
BroadStreetPublishing.com

loved baby: Helping You Grieve and Cherish Your Child
after Pregnancy Loss

ISBN 978-1-4245-5527-7 (hardcover)
ISBN 978-1-4245-5528-4 (e-book)

Stock or custom editions of BroadStreet Publishing titles may be purchased in bulk for
educational, business, ministry, fundraising, or sales promotional use. For information,
please e-mail info@broadstreetpublishing.com.

Cover design by Chris Garborg at garborgdesign.com
Typesetting by Katherine Lloyd at theDESKonline.com

This devotional is the result of a qualitative study undertaken by the author and
presented in the form of this book. The qualitative study explored the emotional experiences of women and men post-pregnancy loss. For more information, please visit the
author's website allamericanmom.net.

Printed in China

18 19 20 21 5 4 3 2

*To my heavenly Father: For teaching me about faith.
This book is completely of you and for you.*

*To my darlings, Titus, Sophie, and Beckham:
I love you. More than you shall ever imagine.*

To my Perry:

*For everything. For believing in me, for loving me,
for being an amazing father and husband, and for telling
me to keep going every time I wanted to call this book quits.
For always you will be mine.*

*To the sweet mamas reading and who have been involved
in this book: This is for your precious arrows in the sky.*

*Give sorrow words:
the grief that does not speak whispers
the o'er-fraught heart and bids it break.*

—William Shakespeare, *Macbeth*

Contents

Introduction

Dear Beloved,

I'm so sorry. Let me offer my sincerest condolences. I wish I could wrap my arms around you. Catch your tears. I've been there. This book includes my journey of loss and hope.

Fellow women have also been there. In these pages, I share the stories of more than forty women, the Loved Baby Tribe. Their voices, echoing tales of stillbirth, miscarriage, and ectopic loss are sprinkled throughout. We want you to feel less alone in this mess of life. We are here for you. You are now a part of a sisterhood: a sisterhood of women whose loved babies were born into the goodness of heaven.

This book is a place for you to mourn and cherish the lovely little life that took root in your womb. This book is for your heart. Other books may care for your physical needs, but this is to cradle the needs of your soul. It is designed with thirty-one devotionals, each with ideas for how to care for yourself and prayers to pray. There is also a special place for you to commemorate your own babe and a place to record your story.

I know this will not abolish the pain, but I want you to be less alone as you mourn, question, and work toward building your strength by drawing closer to God.

The journey brings with it intense emotions. What you are about to read is an honest reflection of loss, but it also includes the hope of tomorrow.

With all my love,
Sarah

Every night I read a bedtime story to my son. When he was twenty-one months old, I invited my husband to snuggle with us for the reading of a new picture book about a daddy bear who spends an idyllic day with his little cub. On the last page of the book I had handwritten a new ending. "Guess what?" it read, "You are going to be a dad to another little cub!"

Perry had been coveting a baby for months. He wanted to be one of those men with a quiver full of arrows—except he described it as wanting a full soccer team. He was over-the-moon excited!

A week or so later, I realized something wasn't right. It was just the first trimester, but my back felt as if it had been slammed with a hammer. I doubled over with what felt like contractions. It was unsettling and didn't feel like my first pregnancy. Too many aches. Too many pains. I called my ob-gyn. "Come on in," the nurse said. Perry abandoned work and drove me. I tried to fix my eyes on the budding trees outside the car window instead of worrying about what I would find at the doctor's office. I spent an hour there. They drew my blood. They checked if I was bleeding. Checked me for a UTI. Nothing wrong could be found. I was released with the consoling words, "Everything will probably be just fine." We traveled home.

As soon as we returned to our farm, I sat at my computer and logged into the one and only distance learning class I took while earning my PhD. My three other group members were already logged in and class was about to begin. "Five minutes till class," typed the instructor. I replied to my instructor and group members, "I might be a little off tonight. My husband and I have been at the doctor with pregnancy complications. The doctor says all is fine, but I'm still exhausted. I apologize in advance if I don't sound as energetic as usual." Quick responses of "congratulations" and "hope all is well" erupted on the screen while I furiously reviewed my notes for our all-important presentation.

I was exhausted but relieved that my doctor said most likely all would be okay. I trusted those words. My backache, pains, and disconcerting feeling were most likely side effects of pregnancy. My nurse had given me a reassuring hug and a send-off of, "Take it easy, and we will call to check on you in the morning." I was at a place of peace.

Then I felt it—the sure sign that everything wasn't fine. I instantly knew I was losing my baby.

Two minutes till the start of class. My thighs warm and wet. I sprinted to the bathroom. I saw the red. I knew my dream had just escaped my body. An arrow darted off through the sunset.

The Bible tells us:

Behold, children are a gift of the LORD,
THE FRUIT OF THE WOMB IS A REWARD.
LIKE ARROWS IN THE HAND OF A WARRIOR,
So are the children of one's youth.
How blessed is the man whose quiver is full of them.
(Psalm 127:3–5 NASB)

I like to imagine I have arrows in the sky. A quiver in heaven.

But it's not that peaceful of a transition, is it? This journey is full of emotional toil. At the time, I didn't know I would be on a journey with other moms who had lost their babies. I never could have imagined the pain and emptiness. But I also didn't know this tragedy would draw me closer to the Lord.

And that is what this book is about—taking steps together to grieve, cherish, and look ahead as we honor our loved babies. It is a place to recount your thoughts and move through the loss rather than stepping over it. Ultimately, we know the Lord holds our hearts and we are never far from his presence and his purposes in our lives. Our stories are all vastly different, but we are united. Sweet mama, this book is dedicated to all our blessed arrows who live amidst the twinkling stars.

Praise be to the God and Father of our Lord Jesus Christ, the Father of compassion and the God of all comfort, who comforts us in all our troubles, so that we can comfort those in any trouble with the comfort we ourselves receive from God.
2 Corinthians 1:3–4

You Are Becoming
a New Creation

A field of perennial wildflowers grows in my front yard. Bright pink, sunny yellow, and vibrant orange beauties wave in the wind. The honeybees from our hives rest upon the delicate petals and soak up the sweet nectar. You see, these lovely flowers are not just eye-catching but bestow life for the bees and crops on our farm. Wildflowers were created to be carefree and grow wherever they are rooted.

We, as sisters in Christ, are much like these wildflowers, aren't we? At our strongest we nurture others and radiate love. We are fetching, glorious creatures. We yearn to grow life and enjoy a carefree existence. But the loss of our baby changes that for us, doesn't it?

Dear mama, you are like this field of wildflowers. You were your bright self when all of a sudden your precious offspring left for heaven. You did nothing to cause this, yet it is far from where you thought your life would be planted in this season. Now you are suffocating. You don't feel or look like your former self, do you? You can barely take care of yourself—much less give life to others.

Your very roots have come undone. You wonder if you will ever emerge from this sadness.

Gather close as I tell you: *You will get to the other side of grief.* You'll go through a frigid winter, but eventually spring will emerge. Just like the wildflowers in my field, you too will gain new strength from your former self and establish new roots and new life. A new you will slowly begin emerging. *How?* you might ask.

God says that we will all be a new creation. Molded into new strength from our suffering.

Yet those who wait for the LORD
Will gain new strength;
They will mount up with wings like eagles,
They will run and not get tired,
They will walk and not become weary.

Isaiah 40:31 NASB

You probably don't see it now. Strength is too far ahead on the horizon, isn't it? That is okay. It can't be rushed, but you will one day arrive. Please know: *arrive* doesn't mean *complete healing* waits on the other side. But the other side is a place where you will not be gasping for every breath, tears unrelenting, thinking constantly of the child you lost. With time, sadness and peace will dance together. Strength will take root deep in your heart. Those of us who have walked a step ahead can tell you that you will be able to sense God's strength over time.

Listen to this promise: "So do not fear, for I am with you; do not be dismayed, for I am your God. I will strengthen you and help you; I will uphold you with my righteous right hand" (Isaiah 41:10).

And he will help you. Call out his name.

Our God says, "I will make rivers flow on barren heights, and springs within the valleys. I will turn the desert into pools of water, and the parched ground into springs" (Isaiah 41:18).

Do you see these promises? God revives. Though your heart is parched, he will replenish your soul. No well is too deep for his love. He turns our weakness into his strength.

Dear one, we who have walked this journey know you are in the midst of terrible darkness. But your very soul is changing toward the light and life he offers. Here is how:

Your heart will be filled with compassion.

This pain will open your heart to suffering. Author Suzanne Eller says, "As you mend, you will discover that you move from needing help to giving it."[1] One day you will use this very suffering to comfort others who are at their weakest.

You'll learn to faithfully accept the life you have been gifted.

Grace says, "Ten years later, I know it was supposed to be part of the story God is writing in our life—even though it was painful. It gave me passion for the preciousness of life."

Your heart will be open to gratitude.

Mia says, "The due date of the baby we lost two years ago was last week. I almost forgot it. That was a mixed emotion. Good because I wasn't grieving as fiercely as I did at the actual due date or even one year later, but sad because I felt like I had forgotten my child for a moment. But I look at my children differently since our loss. I'm so grateful for them in a way I don't think I would have been without our loss."

You will value the sanctity of motherhood.

Camila, an attorney who had a late-term loss, says, "I think going through my loss made me appreciate the sacred calling we have as women to be mothers. I hope when I do have children someday, I will always try to remember that and carry that title of a mother with respect and dignity and not be so flippant about the role that God has blessed me with."

You will have a stronger connection to God.

You might go through times of questioning God and being outright angry, but you can emerge with a stronger relationship. Emalee, who had an ectopic pregnancy, was faced with her own death due to hemorrhaging. Moments before she had to lie on the operating table, she realized she didn't know whether she would go to heaven or hell. Her life changed. She credits the *death* of her child to giving her eternal *life*.

Dear mama, this is *your* path of life. Even though your journey is paved with rocky soil, you must keep marching toward life ahead. I know you wonder how forward is even possible. Right now every single step brims with pain, doesn't it? Brittnie, whose son Chance was born sleeping at five months, says, "The weight you are feeling now does lift. However, you will never be the same. We never move on from our losses, but we do learn how to live a new normal. We can only put our hope in the one who makes all things new."

I want to encourage you—one day your pace will be less arduous. The wildflower within your heart will again blossom, your desert will be refreshed, and one day you will be reunited with your child. Hold to these promises. Look to eternity.

Soul Work

- Choose a Scripture or quote to meditate upon. This will serve as a source of light when that blanket of grief gives you no room to breathe. Mine was, "Be still, and know that I am God" (Psalm 46:10).

- Write the quote on paper. Post it on your mirror. Place it in your car where you will see it. Write it on your hand.

- When you feel that dark suffocation, repeat the verse silently or aloud—whatever you need.

Prayer Time

Lord, my soul is weak. Although I want to cower, I choose to walk in faith, for you are my strength. Although I feel as if I am in a wasteland, I know you created me as a radiant creature. My identity is in you alone. Amen.

Walking in Faith

There I sat on the cold porcelain toilet. Blood pouring. Stomach contracting. I needed no clinician to give me the news; my baby was gone. I was no longer pregnant. I was not going to be decorating a nursery. I was not going to be delivering my baby in November.

It's hard when our world just stops. Nothing makes sense. Fog descends. We feel robbed. Broken. Betrayed by our own bodies.

You might have felt the blood. You might have seen the ultrasound image. You might have heard the devastating phrase, "There is no heartbeat." The nurse might have called and said your HCG was dropping. You might have doubled over in pain from your ectopic pregnancy. Your water might have broken too early. Your baby might have emerged through a caesarean. You might have felt the pains of labor and delivered your perfectly formed baby whose breath was silent.

Our lives changed. Forever.

And we all have different reactions, but most of us report shock and confusion. Amanda, a teacher, says of discovering her loss, "I went from over the moon to on my knees so fast."

Lake says, "Physically the worst was during and just after: cramps. They were worse than any I've had before. Emotionally I had it the hardest when I passed what I believe to be the baby. I said a little prayer and cried. I remember crying a lot that day and the next. I think that transferred to being almost unemotional or numb. It almost felt not real."

Elation can turn into sorrow in a quick, unexpected second, can't it? Even though we find comfort that our babies are in heaven with God, it still hurts.

I'm embarrassed to even speak my truth, but it's mine and I'll say it.

When I realized that my dream had been deferred, I tore off my bloody clothes, put on a pad to catch the remnants of my pregnancy, quickly peered into the toilet, then turned my head away. I almost vomited at the tissue that was floating around. Then I flushed.

I was so unprepared for what happened that I disposed of the signs of my pregnancy. I tried to erase the shame. Then I hobbled back to my computer, still in horrid pain, and led the hour-long presentation on the value of multicultural literature. To this day, neither my instructor nor my classmates know that I suffered a miscarriage during class. I couldn't muster the courage to speak the words. But I did emotionally check out from that class and broke my 4.0. It's the only B on my entire transcript of graduate classes.

Weren't my actions callous? I was so detached from the reality right in front of my face. My mind exploded with shame. Instead of examining and praying over the contents my body had released, instead of breaking down and crying out to God, instead of calling my husband and begging him to come wrap his arms around me, I went back to work. Blood still pouring, I trucked onward. Stomach still contracting, I went on autopilot. It's called denial. Shock. Sometimes our hearts need time to catch up to our reality.

Debra entered the ultrasound room when she was ten-weeks pregnant. She says: "The technician tried several times to locate the baby but couldn't. Then she tried again and there it was. Not nearly as big as it should be. Not moving. Stuck there on the top left of the screen in a huge sac. She didn't really say anything, and I think I asked about something being wrong. She said it so calm and loving, 'Unfortunately, there is no heartbeat.' Then she walked out of the dark room and left our baby's picture frozen on the screen for my husband and me to view. I just lost it. I didn't know what to say, how to feel, what to do. I was numb in so many ways."

Allison says, "I was working alongside my boss the day I started bleeding. I made it through most of the day without him noticing anything was wrong, and then late in the day he looked at me and asked what was wrong. I just broke down. He sent me home and told me to take care of myself and that work would be there when I was ready. He was wonderful. I had just started to get *so* excited about the baby. And, just like that, it was gone."

Denial can also manifest into literally running from reality. Viv, whose loss occurred thirty years ago, vividly remembers the day her world halted. "At four and a half months pregnant," she says, "I started spotting blood—dark, almost black blood. My doctor sent me for an ultrasound. He told me the baby died at eleven weeks! The doctor called my husband to come get me at his office. I was *very* upset! I couldn't sit still and I *ran* out of the office and headed home. I don't remember the drive at all. It was like a bad, bad nightmare."

These feelings of devastation, surprise, and anger after finding out you are losing your baby are common grief reactions.[1]

Forward from Denial: The Many Emotions of Grief

I'm so sorry you are sitting in this nightmare where anger, guilt, sadness, loneliness, yearning, anxiety, and depression swirl. Not to mention you've faced immense physical pain (something we are totally unprepared for).

What are we to do with all this hurt? Are we to push it aside or feel all the feels?

Grief research suggests we must embrace these feelings. There is no way around grief. We must plod right through it. You are sad, you yearn for your child, you want to express yourself, and you yearn to find a meaningful reason.

Have you tried to convince yourself that you shouldn't even grieve? Don't allow this untruth to lead you through this journey. The grief of miscarriage and stillbirth, no matter how early, is the same type of grief that we feel after other losses.[2]

When I am afraid, I put my trust in you.

Psalm 56:3

We must make daily decisions to work through the grief. This doesn't mean there is a *cure* to grief, but it can give us a sense of order to our emotions and help us as we get to a place where sadness and peace coexist. My mother delivered her first child at seven months. He was born sleeping. She says, "The heart-stabbing pain and guilt does go away. Eventually, it will be replaced with loving acceptance and knowledge that you will see each other again in heaven."

Beloved, right now you are still in that raw grief stage. Faith means trusting plans we don't desire. Even though we are afraid, we must trust God to guide us through this valley.

Soul Work

Understanding how we grieve can help us navigate this walk. Turn to the appendix and read further information on how we mourn. Are you surprised by the process? This book is designed to help us walk together through many of these tasks.

Prayer Time

Lord, I am afraid. And my heart aches.
As I walk through this valley of the shadow
of death, I ask you to walk alongside me.
I will trust in you. Amen.

3

Quiet Love: Asking for What You Need

my husband found me burrowed atop our four-poster bed. I had turned off the computer and tucked myself under my white comforter. The bedside lamp flickered beside me. It was the darkest of dark outside. It was the night of my first loss.

Perry and our little man arrived home.

Earlier I'd proudly dressed Titus' little body in his new navy blue shirt with the words "BIG BROTHER" colorfully embroidered across the chest. Now I looked at that shirt with sheer hatred. It was a reminder of what was supposed to be.

Perry already knew the devastating news. I'd frantically called him. "It's over," I'd whispered. "I'm bleeding." A few beats of a second. I hung up the phone.

And now, here he was, peering at me from the doorway. He found me sobbing uncontrollably. I could barely catch a breath between the forceful panting.

The dam called shock and denial had broken; I needed immediate comfort. But I didn't know how to speak my pain. And he didn't know how to speak his pain.

I bet you don't know how to speak your pain either. It's too heavy for words, isn't it?

Well, Perry did the best thing possible in this circumstance. He wrapped his strong arms around my weary body. He held my head as I cried on that bed in our farmhouse. He tussled my hair. He didn't let go.

I don't remember him saying a single word. Maybe he uttered, "I'm so sorry." But that was the extent of our conversation. And to be honest, I didn't want words. I wanted him near, but I wanted quiet. I wanted someone to quietly mourn with me.

Are you at that point? You don't want someone to clamor on and on. Or shoot questions. There is time for that later, but right now you just want everything to hush. Sometimes our souls need quiet. We need the outside world to stop the clatter of talk and the swish of sentences. God explains that we must:

Be still, and know that I am God.

Psalm 46:10

Stopping to be still, and giving in to the sovereignty of our Lord, gives us strength to weather this storm. We must bask in the quiet eye before the hurricane comes back whirling and whirling stronger and stronger.

Have you taken time to be still?

Many women say they need time to reflect, and they also need quiet love from others. Love that reflects the love God has for us. Lake says her best friend, who had been through a miscarriage herself, came to console her. Lake remembers, "She just hugged me and let me cry. No words. She reminded me that I am strong and will get through this."

We need this soft, hushed support.

Marilyn battled painful endometriosis as a young adult. It was four years of IVF, fertility drugs, and surgeries before she and her husband happily gazed in wonder at their first positive pregnancy test. The jubilation was short-lived; at eight weeks, the baby died.

Marilyn dipped into devastation. Some people thought she should just "get over it."

Do you have people saying that? It's hard when others don't understand, isn't it?

One day Marilyn retreated to the quiet of her bedroom. She lay on her bed and cried. After a bit of time, she realized someone was in the room, rubbing and patting her back. You know who was offering this serene action of comfort?

Marilyn's four-year-old niece.

She had tiptoed into her aunt's bedroom, climbed up on the bed, and curled up right beside her. The child never spoke.

It was this quiet comfort, given by a four-year-old, that gave Marilyn the type of support for which she longed. God reveals himself in many ways, doesn't he?

Quiet support was what Job needed too. You know Job? From the Bible? The man who faced every affliction possible? We can identify with him. At one point, after Job's health had been tested, his three friends came to visit him.

Job's friends see their buddy, but they hardly recognize him because he is in such torment. They start to weep.

It's their next step that gives me pause. Instead of trying to tell their friend to *toughen up* or *quit worrying*, the Bible says, "Then they sat on the ground with him for seven days and seven nights. No one said a word to him, because they saw how great his suffering was" (Job 2:13).

Isn't that something? They cried with him and gave him silent support. Later on, they are not so wise in their comfort, but at that moment they didn't try to fix the problem. They did the best thing possible—they showed up.

Have you ached for this type of solace? A warm body beside you. One that doesn't utter words unless you invite them into the dialogue of your soul.

I hope you have that person. I hope you have the opportunity for silence. You might just sit on the couch and watch movie after movie with your husband, or you might go outside and gaze at the clouds set high above the splendor of creation.

Your loved ones—especially the father of your baby—might want to know how they can help ease you. How they can be a friend. Give them permission to sit quietly beside you in your grief. Ask them to hug you and hold you. Please know you might have to ask for this. Don't be ashamed to speak what you need. It's okay to set boundaries, and it's okay to be specific with your requests. Are you a verbal processor?

Don't be afraid to ask a friend to come sit while you talk and cry. Speak your needs.

Grace told her mother-in-law that she was pregnant and miscarrying the same day. "She told me to lie down and rest, and came up and cleaned my house," Grace says. "[It was] a beautiful presence that I needed in that moment, and for the three days that I labored. I will never forget it."

You'll begin to find peace as you allow your loved ones to help meet your needs. But remember it is your heavenly Father who is the supreme giver of comfort. You can find him in the quiet. All you have to do is be still.

Soul Work

Commit to quiet time each day. Whether we are introverts or extroverts, we all must nourish our souls and take time to just be. You probably feel afraid of the future. One way to fight fear is to draw close to our holy Creator. Guard this time. Read, write, pray, or go outside and look at the magnificence of his creation.

Prayer Time

Lord, I know I can find you in the quiet.
My soul aches for this storm to end,
to have never even started. But I know this is where
you have set my anchor. I don't know why, but you—
in your infinite wisdom—do.
I will be still and know. Amen.

He's Got the Whole World in His Hands

eadlines. Goals. Plans. We love order, don't we? Our society helps us (wrongly) believe we can *plan* our families, our maternity leave, and the years between siblings. Pharmaceutical companies burst with pregnancy prevention options. People fight over making *choices*. We talk about *starting a family* as if we are making dinner plans.

Therefore, it must be harder to prevent pregnancy than to *get* pregnant and have a baby. Under the covers and nine months later deliver a baby, right? *Sheesh.*

Did you think you could plan out your life too?

I was a young, idealistic newlywed when my best friend and I put our life agendas on a piece of paper. It was a list (that included specific dates) we could easily, or so we thought, check off. *Graduate with advanced degrees. Get a puppy. Conceive baby. Deliver baby. Maternity leave. Return to teaching.* The most taxing decision was the best month to give birth.

"We'd have a tan in summer," one of us said.

"Yeah, but it's just so darn hot! We'd sweat too much," said the other.

"But I don't want a baby in January. January is peak flu season."

It was just the type of conversation that would make my blood boil today.

Both of us graduated *on time*—check! Got our new puppies *on time*—check! But when it came to conceiving babies, I learned that you can plan and execute all you want, but it is completely up to God whether or not a child is conceived and whether or not you have a healthy, full-term pregnancy. Making babies is not a check-the-box type of endeavor.

I roll my eyes at my blissful ignorance.

We can make our plans,
but the LORD determines our steps.

Proverbs 16:9 NLT

After our losses, many of us are reminded—or find out for the first time—that we aren't actually the ones in control of our lives. This is a hard reality to face, isn't it?

Your pregnancy may have started out either planned or unplanned. But regardless of the beginning, once your eyes spied the positive, you went into overdrive planning and imagining how baby would be incorporated into your life.

You found out you were pregnant with your baby (you might have been nervous, scared, or excited), you used your body to nurture your baby (maybe you bought books, began a Pinterest board, envisioned rocking your little love, started shopping, stopped drinking coffee), and then you lost your baby. Boom. The physicality is quite intense; the emotional toil is real.

Not only do we grieve for our child, but we also grieve because our plans failed. And because we falsely believe we are the ones in control of our lives, we often (wrongly, I must add) feel like a failure. Our soul starts sending out the crushing false message, *My body failed me. I failed our baby!* Our soul screams, *This wasn't part of my plan! I thought this was supposed to be easy! Isn't having a baby a part of happily ever after?*

Those of us who have experienced loss are now changed souls. I am no longer naïve. I gaze at mamas with their swollen bellies and realize the absolute sacredness of what is growing in their bodies.

Oh, how I yearn to be in control.

But I must surrender this desire of control. I am not the one who creates and sustains life.

I am not in control.

You are not in control.

God is in control.

In Romans we read, "And we know that God causes everything

to work together for the good of those who love God and are called according to his purpose for them" (Romans 8:28 NLT).

While fresh in my grief, I was angry and wanted to stomp those words. How can the death of my baby be a part of a grand plan of goodness?

I don't specifically know why a baby perished in my womb. Or why this is a part of your journey. But I also don't know why some women get cancer. Or why a family of five was killed in a car accident last week. All I know is that God created the garden of Eden as pure goodness. But sin got in the way. So perfect goodness cannot be obtained on this earth.

Listen to the gospel: "I have told you these things, so that in me you may have peace. In this world you will have trouble. But take heart! I have overcome the world" (John 16:33).

Do you see that promise? *You will have trouble.* Ouch. You see, our lives are not promised to be pure happiness. We are actually promised lives that are intermixed with troubles. Earth is not the place where pure happiness exists. That is why we long for heaven—a place absent of suffering.

Remember, although your baby died on earth, your baby was born into heaven. Not the plan you would have chosen, but there is an absolute promise for the future—God's master plan—heaven.

It's hard to grasp this promise right now, isn't it? Harper said, "My faith reminds me that I have a specific plan while on this earth. I can endure trials with the Lord. Yet, the emotional side of me wants to panic, cry, and hide in my bed with a pint of ice cream."

In this moment, you are in control of putting your hope in the hands of the Lord. So grab that pint of ice cream and hide in your bed, but trust what Paul says: "I consider that our present sufferings are not worth comparing with the glory that will be revealed in us" (Romans 8:18).

Our heart suffers right now in the present, but there is the promise that one day you will greet your child in the place where glorious happiness shall forever exist. Trust that, "He will wipe every tear from their eyes. There will be no more death or mourning or crying or pain, for the old order of things has passed away" (Revelation 21:4).

Soul Work

Not having control of our lives is challenging. But there are actions we can govern. Choose one or two healthy tasks and accomplish them each day:

- Eat healthier.
- Go to bed at the same time each night.
- Get fresh air.
- Drink eight glasses of water per day.
- Go outside to stargaze.
- Take a nightly bubble bath.
- Read the Bible each day.

Taking charge of a self-care habit will help your mind focus on the task at hand while you put the rest in the Lord's hands.

Prayer Time

Lord, grant me the serenity to accept the things I cannot change, courage to change the things I can, and wisdom to know the difference. Amen.

(From the "Serenity Prayer" by Reinhold Niebuhr.)

Searching for Why

Shannon and her husband had been trying to conceive for months. On Christmas Eve, they discovered their dream had come true! But the excitement soon ended. On New Year's Eve Shannon went to the restroom. She says, "There was a sack/balloon in the toilet. I panicked. I made Blake grab my phone, so I could call the doctor while still on the toilet. They told me to stay calm and describe what I saw. Describe it? I was horrified! They scheduled an appointment for eleven that morning and told me to stay in bed until I got there.

"I had to call my mom to ask for my blood type. She thought it a strange question to ask, especially since I was in tears. I told her that I was pregnant but we thought we were losing the baby. After an hour's drive, I had an ultrasound that confirmed I had been pregnant (my uterus was swollen) but I had miscarried (my uterus was empty). I bawled on the ultrasound table. Blake did all he could to keep me calm, but there was nothing he could do. He cried too, which actually made me feel better. When I saw the doctor, she examined me and told us there was nothing we could do; miscarriages happen more often than people think.

"I couldn't believe *it* had happened. As much as she told me it wasn't my fault, I kept trying to figure out what went wrong. *What had I done?*"

Asking God Why

Oh beloved, why explodes in all our minds, doesn't it? Why sabotages our personal narrative. Was it something I ate? Is God punishing me? Is it because I wasn't immediately happy to be pregnant? Is it because I tried to wish away my pregnancy? Was I not a good enough mother?

In the next devotional, we will explore the medical aspect of why, but right now let's look at the spiritual.

After my first miscarriage, I huddled in bed with my laptop and a cup of tea as companions. I searched for *why* like I was in hot pursuit of the Holy Grail, except my archaeological dig site was the Internet.

First I investigated the physical causes. Although I read that most miscarriages are caused by chromosomal abnormalities, I had a hard time trusting that information.[1] Are you sure it wasn't the coffee I drank last week? *Nope.* Or that hot dog from the birthday party? *Nope.* Was it that one glass of wine before I knew I was pregnant? *Still nope.*

Then my mind took me down the rabbit hole of spirituality. In the beginning disbelief numbed. But gradually (maybe overnight), it turned to the elixir of anger at myself and at God. *Why God? Why? Why! How could you do this to me?*

You might sympathize. After a loss, we immerse ourselves in these questions. Then we find ourselves further baffled. And full of guilt. We wonder, *Is it okay for a Christian to question God? Am I a bad person to feel angry at him? Is he punishing me?*

Are you asking those questions?

You are not alone. Don't be ashamed. You are not a weak Christian for these emotions. This theological question is something most of us ask. And anger, even at our heavenly Father, is something that has sprung from deep within most of our souls.

I want to share with you what I learned in hopes that it might help quiet your heart.

The loss we have endured is not a consequence of sin.

Look at the Bible. Jesus was perfect. He committed no sin. The Bible says, "He committed no sin, and no deceit was found in his mouth" (1 Peter 2:22). Jesus never sinned, yet he suffered. You see, in this world we will all suffer. Good and bad happens to *all* of us. The Bible explains, "He causes his sun to rise on the evil and the good, and sends rain on the righteous and the unrighteous" (Matthew 5:45). The Bible is clear:

the loss of our little one is not because of any sin we have conducted, nor would it have been prevented had we been perfect. Grasp these truths if you feel as if you did something spiritually to cause the loss of your child.

Prayer is a conversation with God, and sometimes that conversation is heated.

The Bible provides us instance after instance of people lamenting their concerns to God. There is none more profound than Jesus hanging on the cross: "About three in the afternoon Jesus cried out in a loud voice, '*Eli, Eli, lema sabachthani?*' (which means 'My God, my God, why have you forsaken me?')" (Matthew 27:46).

Jesus felt abandoned. You probably feel abandoned. In his forsakenness, he cried out to our heavenly Father. *Why me?*

Jesus felt cast aside. Do you see what he did? He talked with God directly, and he even asked the question that is on all our minds. Asking *why* is not a sin. However, please know that God won't answer in the way we prefer. There won't be a big CNN special or writing in the sky. In fact, God might never answer this question while we are on earth. This is hard to accept.

You might find a medical reason why your baby died; however, you are not promised you will find a spiritual answer. Instead we must trust that God's grand plan is the right one. As Philip Yancey says, "Faith means believing in advance what only makes sense in reverse."[2]

And as we talk to God, grappling with these issues and laying our hurt at his feet, we must be real. We must unburden our hearts. Praying will not reverse the course of action, but it will pour comfort onto our broken hearts and in the process change us.

Grief causes us to question. To dig deep in our faith. Go ahead and ask God those hard questions, but then follow the questioning with prayer, digging into the Word, wise counsel, and being still in his presence. Suffering can be redemptive if we allow it to prompt us to draw closer to God and become more Christlike.

Changing Your Question

Our goal is to replace the wording of our question. You might not be able to today, but you will eventually find yourself or force yourself to be at a place where you stop asking *why* and instead ask *what now*. Ask yourself, *How can I use this to glorify God and become more Christlike?*

You might find that comforting others, cherishing each day, and submitting and trusting his will are all parts of your *what now*.

God is within her, she will not fall;
God will help her at break of day.

(Psalm 46:5)

God can help us with the unimaginable if we call on him. Sharron says, "We were blessed with a beautiful baby girl with our first pregnancy. Two years later, we struggled with secondary infertility. My second pregnancy resulted in our first loss: an ectopic pregnancy. I understood the physical reason for *why*. Several months later I conceived again, but this also resulted in a loss at eighteen weeks. Then I began frantically searching for a physiological reason. Months of genetic testing did not bring us answers. The following year I conceived our son. He became our third loss when he was stillborn. I needed to know what was wrong. I kept believing there was an answer hidden somewhere in my body. I never questioned God, asking *why*. I know that this season of my life taught me to trust God unconditionally. I learned to better submit to his will. Two years and two pregnancy losses later, we found our answer to *why*. A team of fabulous perinatologists diagnosed a condition, prescribed the correct medications, and in less than a year we brought home our miracle baby boy."

Sweet mama, although arduous, we must strive to live out life post-loss like Sharron—trusting unconditionally. We live in a broken world, but God promises to take hold of our broken hearts.

Soul Work

- Asking *why* is normal. Verbalize this question. Write a letter to God. Ask him *why*. Then, when you are ready, submit these questions to him. Hand them over. Beg of him to help you develop unconditional trust.

- Study the book of Job to see that sometimes God doesn't answer *why*. What is your *what now*?

Prayer Time

Lord, why is consuming me. Please help me take these unanswerable questions and turn them into an opportunity for what now. Amen.

Seeking
Medical Answers

One of the many questions that dart over and over in our minds is: *Why did this medically occur?* In the last devotional, we explored the concept of *why* on a spiritual plane. Now we are going to explore how we should search for medical answers.

Whether we have a miscarriage, stillbirth, or an ectopic pregnancy, losing a baby can be, as Cayci says, "the hardest day of my life." We naturally want answers to our questions. Sifting through reputable sources can be comforting because true facts about pregnancy loss always lead you back to a core statement that most likely *you* did *nothing* to cause the loss of your baby.

Please note that conclusive answers of *why* cannot usually be offered with early pregnancy loss. Most often miscarriage is a "random event" when an "embryo receives an abnormal number of chromosomes."[1] At times, though (most common with a stillbirth), testing might reveal a specific cause, which can be anything from an infection to a difficulty with the cord. Information, in this regard, can be powerful because it provides us with empirical evidence that we are not at fault, and although it doesn't diminish the pain of now, it often offers hope for the future.

Only a small percentage of women (1 percent) have repeated miscarriages.[2] In the case of miscarriage, healthcare providers usually begin extensive testing after a woman has had two or more miscarriages. I know this seems a bit unfair. If you want, you can request that your physician expedite this process. Testing began on me after my second miscarriage. It was then that I found out I had PCOS (Polycystic

Ovary Syndrome) and was able to take charge of my own health decisions. But sometimes answers aren't found.

Autopsies are often offered to parents of babies who have been born
past twenty weeks. This testing may or may not offer answers, and it's
often a shock to find out you have to make a financial decision of this
magnitude right on the spot.

Emily says about her search for answers, "I spent most of my time
for days after my miscarriage reading about miscarriage: blogs, articles,
etc. I didn't know anything about miscarriage. I think my miscarriage fell into the 'unknown' category. I had a successful ultrasound
with a strong heartbeat but eventually miscarried. Of course, I wanted
to blame myself. I blamed stress at work because I had been working
eighty hours a week immediately prior to my miscarriage. I blamed
myself for not taking care of my body and for eating turkey sandwiches
without heating up that darn lunchmeat (which I still think is ridiculous). After speaking with my doctor and reading article after article, I
started to reassure myself it wasn't my fault. My doctor never told me it
was my fault or there was a problem with me, so until someone told me
I couldn't or shouldn't conceive again, I was going to keep trying. I will
say that what helped me was the fact that I read several articles that
indicated most people go on to have a healthy pregnancy after a loss.
I focused on that and tried not to concentrate on the 'what if' until it
applied to me."

Information can also make us confused. We crave answers and like
to know the cause of an effect. At times, our search leads us to a place
where there is no explainable reason. Camila, who had a late-term loss,
says it was maddening to not know the cause even after her baby had an
autopsy. "I was so confused. I consoled myself by thinking, *Maybe this
is for the best, maybe something was wrong with the baby and it just couldn't
handle living in this world.* But this backfired because I had a follow-up
appointment with the doctor, and she told me all the tests came back
showing my baby was perfect and nothing was abnormal. So I went all
the way back through the blaming myself all over again. I finally gave

up. She told me that even doctors usually do not have answers. I still struggle with this."

At this point, we must pray that we can surrender our need for an explanation. We must reconcile that we might not know why from a spiritual or a medical standpoint.

But we do know specific things that do not cause pregnancy loss. Exploring what doesn't cause pregnancy loss can help negate the guilt that sometimes holds our souls captive.

What Doesn't Cause Pregnancy Loss

Many people make false assumptions about the causes of pregnancy loss. A national survey revealed that 76 percent of respondents thought the cause of miscarriage was a stressful event, 74 percent thought the cause of a miscarriage to be long-standing stress, 64 percent falsely thought that lifting a heavy object could cause a miscarriage, 41 percent thought a sexually transmitted disease was a factor, 31 percent believed an abortion could contribute to future pregnancy loss, 28 percent thought the use of implanted long-term birth control could cause miscarriage, and 23 percent thought because a woman did not want the baby that she might miscarry.[3] Wow! These untrue assumptions reveal society's ignorance about miscarriage.

You too might have thought that one of the above reasons caused your loss. Please know that none of the above statements have any medical bearing on the viability of a pregnancy. Nor does moderate caffeine consumption (less than 200 mg per day).[4]

Guilt, especially self-blame, is a common emotion post-miscarriage. We think we could have protected our baby. I want you to know that the death of your baby wasn't because you picked up your thirty-pound toddler when he wanted a hug, or because you were stressed because of financial matters, or because you drank a cup of coffee that morning. Please try to combat your misguided guilt with the truth of the matter. You see, even if we do everything right, the viability of our child is totally out of our hands. God is in control of our lives. Our job is to make sure our bodies are as healthy as possible and then give the rest to God.

Consider the Source

It is important that we have accurate information from reputable sources. You might have just been told that you have PCOS, endometriosis, or any other number of factors that might have contributed to your loss. Knowledge about our specific loss and our health will help us engage in conversations with our health provider, move us forward with our grief, make future health plans, and sort through the confusion in our minds.

But take caution. The advent of online resources means that misinformation and misguided opinions are readily available; I urge you to always consider the source as you search for further information.

Here are some tips as you seek information:

1. Your healthcare provider might have sent you home with pamphlets. Start there. If you can't find them or if you didn't receive them, call your provider to see if they will give you sources.
2. If you search online, please know the difference between research and opinion. When our hearts ache, it can be difficult to make that distinction. Message boards and support groups can provide community, but don't take everything you read on the sites as the truth. Seek out the primary source of the opinion.
3. Rely heavily on bulletins and information from the American College of Obstetrics and Gynecology.
4. Rely heavily on the March of Dimes. Not only does this organization provide factual information, but this group also takes in the needs of the bereaved parents by using terminology such as "baby" instead of "tissue."

5. Ask your healthcare provider. Take your questions to the expert. If you are uneasy with the answers, do not hesitate to seek a second opinion.

Dear one, sometimes we just don't have an answer. Spiritually or medically. And it compounds the problem when the innocent question of "So what happened?" sends daggers to our hearts, because we wrongly feel that we must be to blame. But it is not our fault. Not one single bit. Please don't let the ignorance of people or the whispers of satan cause you any additional turmoil. Cling to medical truths and rest in the Spirit.

Maybe you didn't have a caring healthcare team. The office that took care of me was wonderful and nurturing. Not everyone is so fortunate. Many women are delivered the devastating news in very clinical and abrupt terms. If you feel uncomfortable with the team that is taking care of you, seek help elsewhere. You don't want to carry that bitter baggage with you as you continue your health journey. We must be advocates for our own health.

Soul Work

Do you have answers to your loss? Do you have further questions? Write them down. Schedule a time to speak with your healthcare provider or conduct preliminary research from reputable sites.

Prayer Time

Lord, I pray I can surrender control of knowing why my loss happened. Father, please guide the physicians as they guide me. Amen.

Meet Hannah:
Our Biblical Soul Mate

annah cried. She wept. Month after month. Year after year. Salty tears spilled. She couldn't eat. Her heart grieved. The life-giving part of her body—her womb—was closed.

Elkanah, her husband, didn't understand her suffering. "Why are you crying, Hannah?" Elkanah would ask. "Why aren't you eating? Why be downhearted just because you have no children? You have me—isn't that better than having ten sons?" (1 Samuel 1:8 NLT).

He continually questioned why she was sad and not eating. He didn't understand this yearning that couldn't be quenched.

A mother. That is what Hannah wanted to be. Although her husband doted on her and loved her, his culture dictated he marry another so he could have a family. Hannah was unable to provide children, so he took an additional wife.

Then, as if her barrenness were not punishment enough, as if seeing her husband's new wife give birth to numerous precious babies were not anguish enough, the new wife purposefully provoked Hannah. "So Peninnah would taunt Hannah and make fun of her because the Lord had kept her from having children" (1 Samuel 1:6 NLT).

Bless Hannah's soul. How much more pain could she endure? She was beyond tormented. First Samuel 1:10 says, "Hannah was in deep anguish, crying bitterly as she prayed to the Lord" (NLT). Hannah was humiliated, felt shame, was jealous, lost her appetite, had a husband who didn't understand, was full of bitterness, and cried uncontrollably. Does this sound familiar? It depicts my life after my losses, and I imagine it is a pretty close depiction of yours too.

You see, "Hope deferred makes the heart sick, but a longing fulfilled is a tree of life" (Proverbs 13:12). Hannah had a sick heart; her longing for a baby to cradle in her arms had not been fulfilled.

Your heart is sick right now, isn't it?

Hannah's story is like so many of ours—she is our biblical soul mate. Although our stories are distinctly different, those of us who have had miscarriages, late-term loss, or battled infertility can understand the longing of Hannah. Our hearts have ached, our lives have changed, and we find others don't quite understand the torment.

Sweet Hannah, who lived more than nine hundred years before Christ, could probably sit with us and cry over a cup of tea as we recount our stories. I imagine we would have much in common with this female biblical great who at one time was full of great anguish and sorrow.

I can't tell you how I wept upon discovering this account in the Bible. Seeing how much space was devoted to chronicling Hannah's sadness over not being able to provide a child for herself and her husband offered relief. It was the cold drink of water I needed.

It made me feel less alone.

The verses showed me God recognizes this unmet longing for a child in our arms as a reason worthy of tears and anguish. Hannah's despair is featured in the Bible. To me, this authenticates our sadness and gives us the ultimate permission to cry out to God and express our fullest emotions.

Hannah moaned, howled, ugly-cried to God. Have you done this yet? Squalled those tears and screamed those horrid cries?

Did you know it is okay to direct these emotions at God? Crying in sorrow is a way of communicating and talking to him when our souls are seared with pain.

Lynda wrongly thought after her miscarriage, "God must not want me to have a child. I must not be good enough to be a mom." Each day for four years, Lynda would fall to her knees, cry tears, and beg God for a child. Throughout her turmoil, she put her faith in the Lord and realized that he had a specific story for her life.

God has a specific story for each and every one of our lives. And while we are living out this particular chapter of our story, it is okay to be sad and to cry. It's also normal to cry out to God in bitterness. But we must call on our Father. We must pray. We must seek him.

Then you will call on me and come and pray to me, and I will listen to you. You will seek me and find me when you seek me with all your heart.

Jeremiah 29:12–13

Hannah's story progressed to the birth of a son, whom she named Samuel, "because I asked the LORD for him" (1 Samuel 1:20).

Sweet mama, I don't how your story or mine will progress, but I do know our heavenly Father hears our cries. The grief you feel right now is a universal experience. Grief over the desire for motherhood transcends time and is so important that it is featured in the Bible. We shouldn't be ashamed of our emotions of anger, jealousy, and sadness. Instead we should cry out to the Lord and express our inner turmoil.

This is a type of intimate, personal relationship that we were designed to have with God. Don't try to hide your emotions. Instead pour out your heart. He can handle it.

- Read 1 Samuel 1. Underline the words that describe how you feel. For example, her sorrow is described as *deep anguish*. Do you feel anguish? Have you poured out your soul to the Lord?

- Look back over the words you have underlined. Isn't it remarkable how grief and sadness over an unborn child are universal feelings that transcend time?

- Give yourself permission to pour out your soul to God. The priest, who watched Hannah cry, thought she was drunk she was so distraught. It's okay to be distraught. Grief must be grieved.

Prayer Time

*Lord, listen as I pour out
my heart to you. I ...*

Blessed Are Those Who Mourn: You Are Allowed to Be Sad

eath Becomes Her: A Century of Mourning Attire was recently on display at the Metropolitan Museum of Art.[1] I virtually toured the fascinating bereavement ensembles of the nineteenth and early twentieth century. Stark black dresses, hats, and jewelry. The heft and color of the dresses corresponded to the level of grief felt by the lady whose heart was troubled.

Did you know the tradition of clothing yourself to express sorrow actually harkens to biblical times? "Then Jacob tore his clothes, put on sackcloth and mourned for his son many days" (Genesis 37:34). Sackcloth was the original black funeral dress.

Our modern times don't dictate appropriate costume for the period of grief.

But we feel like we are clothed in that itchy sackcloth, don't we? We feel the heft of grief, the constant pricking of it on our souls, the veil that disjoints our very view. The difference between times of old and today is that the outward sign of grief has been removed. Our grief cloaks only our souls.

I'm not suggesting we revive the tradition of mourning attire, but it is rather nice to know how historically there was an outward sign saying, *Hey, I'm hurting over here. Let me cry. Pray for me. Don't forget me.*

Harper, a university professor, says, "I remember after my miscarriage, I was trying to be brave, and my husband looked at me and said, 'You're allowed to be sad. You're allowed to be angry.'"

We should all follow this advice. Even though our culture doesn't give us protocol, we must give ourselves permission to mourn.

Blessed are those who mourn,
for they will be comforted.

Matthew 5:4

Examine this Scripture. Mourning must come before comfort. Mourning is a biblical process of coping. Others might minimize our sorrow, but the Bible tells us we are called to mourn. Abraham mourned the loss of his wife. Warrior David cried. Our very Savior Jesus wept. And you too must settle in for a time of mourning.

Unfortunately many of us feel confusion. Katie recalls, "I had at least one confirmed miscarriage and only recently came to understand that everything I went through—the guilt, depression, etc.—wasn't me 'overreacting' or being hormonal. I tried to marginalize my feelings, because I felt no one would understand."

Rachel, a labor and delivery nurse, says, "Losing Brooklyn and Brianna at nineteen weeks was the worst experience I have ever been through. Having to lie in that bed in labor knowing I would be leaving the hospital without my babies was unexplainable pain."

Unexplainable pain must be grieved. Beloved, mourning is normal and necessary. Don't cover the fount when grief needs to well up in your soul. Some of you have this dam built up. Release it. Some of you are pouring like it will never end. Feel it.

Lynda, after years of infertility and loss, was surprised to learn she was again pregnant. She considered this "a blessing from God!" They had conceived this baby the old-fashioned way, "without all the planning, counting days, and taking temperatures!" She and her husband were overjoyed to see the heartbeat of the baby on the monitor at six weeks.

During the twelfth week, they found the heart of the baby no longer beat. Lynda says, "The nurse's words were in a whisper: 'I'm sorry, I want you to know you can call me personally anytime if you need to talk.' She was a stranger to me, but so compassionate. My husband and I sat silent—silent tears, silent pain, and silent stares. We silently walked to the car. The silence was so thick that I don't even remember the car starting or the engine running. He drove to the river dam and parked. I zoned out, watching the water rush. He stepped out of the car and disappeared. I worried about his whereabouts. I walked around, half-heartedly looking for him. When I found him, he was standing still, shoulders hunched, with a sheet of tears covering his face. He was like a statue. There was a void between us. We could not even embrace each other. I don't remember getting home. At home, all the lights were left off. The silence followed us through the rooms. My head throbbed. Our pastors visited, and I could barely break through the silence to say, 'Thank you for coming.' Scott spoke to them and they left. At bedtime, he stood at the doorway to the living room, 'Come on, honey. Let's go upstairs to bed.' I tried to stand to walk but collapsed in a burst of screaming sounds of despair. The sorrow was overwhelming. I had no strength to stand. My silence broke and a loud weeping poured out. My husband tried to catch me as I plunged to the floor, but my body was so limp. He picked me up and carried me up the stairwell to the bedroom. He laid me in the bed and stroked my hair as we both sobbed ourselves to sleep."

There is a period of deep mourning for us all. A period where we feel every prick. I'm not sure how long it will last for you. A month. Six months. A year. We are all different.

The women in the MET exhibit dressed in mourning for a year. Of course, I'm sure some wished to discard that darkness earlier and some wanted to wear it longer. But there is a season of mourning, and eventually we all get to the place where we clothe ourselves in a reflection of our inner selves: a self where sadness and joy coincide.

Dear one, one day you will cast off that sackcloth from your soul.

Soul Work

Dear heart, part of our sadness is that the dreams we had for the future have now come undone. What were your dreams? Go ahead and write them down or talk to God about them. Write a letter to your Loved Baby. Unpack these thoughts, so they don't hold you captive. Your dreams were wonderful, and they deserve to be shared and remembered.

Prayer Time

Lord, I know there is "a time to weep, and a time to laugh; a time to mourn, and a time to dance" (Ecclesiastes 3:4 KJV). Right now my grief feels so heavy. Please help me weep and mourn so my expression of sorrow will give way one day to laughing and feeling joy in my soul. Amen.

When You Go through Deep Waters: Depression and Anxiety

ourning is painful, isn't it? And it makes you feel a bit crazy on the inside. You probably wonder, *What is normal? Are these nightmares something most experience? Will my appetite ever return or get smaller? How do I know if I am suffering from depression or PTSD?* Sweet one, I am not a clinician, but here are some things to know.

What Are the Normal Grief Reactions?

Normal grief reactions include: sleep disturbances, appetite disturbances, absentminded behavior, social withdrawal, distressing dreams, avoiding things that trigger painful feelings, sighing, restless hyperactivity, crying, and treasuring objects that remind you of your little one. Self-blame and a tendency to blame the father of your child is also a specific attribute of miscarriage and stillbirth.[1] Have you felt any of these feelings yet?

The American College of Obstetricians and Gynecologists reminds us, "You need to heal both physically and emotionally. For many parents, emotional healing takes a good deal longer than physical healing. Grief can involve a whole wide range of feelings. You may find yourself searching for a reason your pregnancy ended. You may wrongly blame yourself. You may have headaches, lose your appetite, feel tired, or have trouble concentrating and sleeping."[2]

Truly, we can't avoid these pains. We can take measures to cope, but we can't erase. With God beside us, we can walk forward.

For with God nothing shall be impossible.

Luke 1:37 KJV

Throughout this book we will continue to look at ways to cope. But know you are not the only woman who is carrying around a teddy bear to remember your little love or trying to avoid the sight of other pregnant women. We all have different coping mechanisms.

When Will Grief End?

This question is tricky. Irving Leon, a psychologist who specializes in reproductive loss says, "The overwhelming symptoms of grief usually lessen within nine months to a year. Initially it may feel like a tsunami, and waves of grief come one right after the other. But after a while, they are less intense and less frequent."[3]

Worden tells us, though, that asking when grief will end is a bit like asking, "How high is up?"[4] It can't be answered. However, he says that some evidence of getting to the other side of grief is when we can think of the deceased without pain (sadness, yes, but not that intense physical pain of fresh, cutting grief) and that we are able to reinvest our emotions into other people and into living.

Sweet one, this gap in your soul is never going to be filled. You will always feel pain, but the hard winter of it will one day end. You'll revisit the grief at times, but you won't be trapped forever in the blizzard of your emotions.

When Will I Be the "Old Me"?

Go ahead and discard the idea of the "old you." Let me be the first to welcome you to your new normal. Your eyes will see differently. You might act differently. Before my first loss, I was a bit of a rigid mama to my firstborn. After experiencing loss, I loosened up and started letting us enjoy life together. Eating ice cream cones and dancing to the music while watching *Robin Hood* became hallmarks of the new me. I am also petrified of sudden death, so I had to learn to cope with these feelings.

Worden says, "Mourning is a long-term process and . . . the culmination will not be a pre-grief state.[5] We will be the same, but a bit different. And this is okay.

How Do I Know if I Need Further Help?

How do we know if we need to reach beyond our circle? There should be no stigma for the Christian woman who needs to visit a counselor or who might need to reset a chemical imbalance with medication. Tara says, "I was devastated. I slipped into a deep depression and words cannot express how I was feeling. I had to be sedated when I was told." Depression, anxiety, and PTSD can happen to us all. You know your own story. You know your own trauma. It can range from seeing the toilet to experiencing labor. This is a hard lot to process. Please read these gentle words from a counselor and evaluate whether you might need further assistance post-loss:

> Many times, the catalyst for seeking counseling is when we lose someone or something important to us or when something traumatic transpires in our lives. Pregnancy loss is *both* of these in one devastating occurrence. To need counseling is not only normal but is oft times necessary to cope. Some of the specific signs women might experience are feeling uncontrollable anger, sadness, and/or hopelessness. Sometimes, symptoms of depression, anxiety, or PTSD can manifest in ways that may not appear so clear such as fatigue, eating or sleeping far more or far less than typical, feelings of disengagement in aspects of life that she once enjoyed such as her work, hobbies, activities with her family, etc. Some or all of these feelings are expected post-loss initially, but as time passes and the symptoms don't dissipate or gradually ease, that's a sign that counseling might be needed in order to help you heal. Furthermore, women post-loss might feel detached from their other children initially, but if this continues for an extended period of time, that is a sign of depression.

Again, many of these symptoms are common post-loss, but if they continue to persist several months post-loss, it is recommended that we seek help. No woman post-loss should have to be a shell of the woman she once was, consumed with grief, depression, trauma, and anxiety. There is hope, there is healing, and there is the very same strong, resilient woman we've missed waiting to emerge from the pain. Sometimes, she just needs a little help getting there, and that is perfectly okay.[6]

My Experience with Anxiety

I dealt with anxiety. A few months after my first miscarriage, we saw a positive pregnancy test. My due date would be my husband's birthday! I was so excited to be giving him such a gift. Tentative hopefulness. I felt strong. I felt healthy. I felt as if God was on my side. The first was a statistical fluke. It couldn't happen again.

Although early, we decided to announce our joy to my family. My brother and his wife were visiting, and we all headed off toward the river. We boarded the boat and set out for a day in the sun. I was nervous about announcing our pregnancy, but I wanted to celebrate the child growing inside of me. The pontoon was running full speed ahead when I abruptly yelled, "Stop the boat!" Dad pulled the throttle back, and everyone quizzically looked at me. I took a deep breath. "Guess what Perry is getting for his birthday? A new baby!" My family jumped with joy. They had shared in our sadness and were now happy to share in our new joy. They enveloped us in hugs. I saw tears in their eyes: tears of joy and tears of fear.

Glee. Sadness. Grief. Days after announcing my pregnancy, my doctor called and told me my blood levels were not favorable. Because I'd had a previous miscarriage, my obstetrician was monitoring my HCG levels through biweekly blood work. She whispered another miscarriage was probable. Knowing that it was coming was in a way easier than being surprised, but to realize that life was dying inside my body was devastating. Once again, in my reality I'd failed as a vessel for my unborn child and as a mother. My mother-in-law came to watch my son, so my husband and I could travel to my doctor's office. I felt like a rag doll—empty on the inside.

My friends and family knew I was experiencing a second miscarriage. In my altered reality, I kept thinking they were looking at me as if I were to blame. Underneath their sympathetic words, I imagined all the things they were saying to themselves and to each other behind closed doors. "It was all her fault," I imagined them saying. "She drinks so much coffee," or "She is just so weak." My family's implications that I needed to slow down made me infer they thought the miscarriage was completely my fault because of the stress I had allowed in my life. I was ashamed to be around people because I felt everyone was judging me. I was paranoid. I felt guilty for mourning. My mom had experienced a stillbirth, and my mother-in-law had lost two children. It made me question whether my grief was real and worthy of tears. So I tried to be strong and not grieve. After extensive testing I was told that I had Polycystic Ovary Syndrome (PCOS) and that I might never be able to have children again because my ovaries were unhealthy. I was now quietly mourning the loss of the two babies and the loss of any future babies. My anxiety grew, but with the help of God, I trod through the deep.

Soul Work

Identify the parts of grief you are experiencing. Write them down and ask friends and family to specifically pray for God to help you fight these feelings. Grief tries to convince us that we are to blame or that we are not strong. But you are strong. God is within you.

Prayer Time

As you seek peace during the day and night, you can practice the powerful act of meditative breathing. Breathe in: Emmanuel. Breathe out: God is with me. Do this over and over as you center your mind.

Laughter through the Tears

*et's pause from talking about grief to look at laughter through our tears.

On one of my first visits to a new hairdresser, I whispered, "My hair is falling out. I think it's because of my miscarriage. I guess my hormones are still changing." Outside of my tribe of close friends, I hadn't spoken the words "I had a miscarriage" aloud. But here I was spilling my soul to Ashleigh, the hairdresser. So cliché, right? But I felt like I owed her an explanation for my balding.

To make matters worse, I was turning thirty. Middle-age balding—check. Miscarriage—check. And I had a broken nose. Why? Well, my son collided with my nose when he was diving in to give me a hug. Which meant the romantic dinner and spa date my husband was taking me on for my dirty thirty was a no-go because blood poured from my nostrils. Winner, winner, chicken dinner!

When the time came for me to celebrate at my parents' house, I was in a funk. But when I opened the gift bag my mom handed me with a big smirk on her face, I burst out laughing. And cried tears of hilarity as I placed that long, blonde, bodacious wig on my head and started striking vogue poses. It felt so good to laugh at my situation instead of wallowing in the madness of it all.

There is a line in the movie *Steel Magnolias* that says, "Laughter through tears is my favorite emotion."[1] You see, saving the sanity of our souls sometimes means we must search for joy—even in less than joyful times. I know you grieve, but I want you to not feel guilty for putting a smile on your face right now. You've probably already had it happen.

Something strikes you as funny, you smile, and then you feel instant guilt because you are mourning. Let me tell you something—when it comes to grief, laughter and crying don't have to be mutually exclusive. You will feel both of these emotions during this journey. Laughing doesn't mean you don't miss and mourn for your loved baby. We will feel sad at times and happy at times. It's a strange dance. Just like you have to give yourself permission to grieve, you need to give yourself permission to feel the emotion of happiness.

Laughter is not going to take away the pain, but it will help you get through the pain. Laughter can improve our overall attitude, reduce stress and tension, promote relaxation, improve sleep, help strengthen our relationships, and produce a general sense of well-being.[2] We can all use assistance in any of the above categories.

Laughter can also be a coping mechanism, so we can view situations that trigger negative emotions through the lens of humor. Camila tells me that after her stillbirth a coworker told her that her baby was going to come back as a butterfly. Camila didn't necessarily agree with what her Hindu coworker was telling her. However, she says that instead of being offended, she just accepted the advice and smiled to herself. She found it to be a beautifully touching gesture.

When Amber offered me her uterus after my second miscarriage, I was genuinely hurt. The first miscarriage she brought me cupcakes, but this time she offered me her body. I took it as a sign that she blamed me for my two losses. She was clearly blaming my female parts, right? Looking back, that was so far from the truth. It was one of the absolute kindest gestures anyone made, but in the moment it infuriated me. She didn't let it go either. She wanted me to know that she was serious about being a surrogate if I couldn't bear children.

One hot summer day things got spicy. We were standing on the dock with our fishing poles in the river when she casually reminded my husband and me that we could use her uterus. Again, I felt she was blaming me. In a moment that I am not proud of I turned, glared, pointed at her husband, Jason, and said, "Maybe I just need your husband's sperm.

Maybe, just maybe, it's not *my* uterus's fault but it's Perry's sperm." With that I stomped up the stairs of our wooden dock and went to sit in the hammock. Cue the awkward crickets chirping. But things got a bit more intense. My best friend in the entire world joined us for a BBQ at the river that afternoon. She broke down in tears and apologized to me because she hadn't offered me her uterus first. She cried, "If anyone was going to be carrying your baby, it should be me! I'm your best friend. I'm sorry I didn't offer first."

Things had gotten way out of hand. Number one: I didn't want a surrogate. Number two: I realized my life had become inspiration for a great sitcom sketch or reality show. My best friend was crying because our mutual friend had offered her uterus first, my parents were on the sidelines watching all this unfold, and I had just asked our friend's husband if I could have his sperm—all the while blaming my husband for our losses. Bless.

I look back and laugh. And thankfully, in the moment, I started laughing too. How ridiculous! And how incredibly sweet are my friends? They didn't know how to navigate my loss any better than I did. All this illustrated the full range of their friendship and how my loss affected their lives too.

I want you to laugh too—even if it means finding the dark humor in a horrible situation.

So here are my suggestions:

- Watch a funny movie.
- Go on a childlike date with your hubby or friend. Who doesn't laugh putting on bowling shoes or falling down while ice skating? My best friend took me on a girl's weekend. We sat by the pool and read books. When a rainstorm threatened to halt our fun, we ran up the steps to the waterslide and whizzed down the slide through the showers.
- Ask your friends to send you funny memes. Friends are always looking for ways to help. Contact them and let them

know you would appreciate them sending you funny messages, e-mails, or texts to help you smile during the day.

- Watch hilarious YouTube videos or check out the latest upload to humor websites. Google "people of Walmart." Trust me. You will laugh.
- If you want to be around people but don't want that awkward silence that accompanies it all, host a party. If the holidays have you down, have your group of friends come over in their tackiest sweaters. Or host a board game night. Charades can help anyone's soul.

Sweet lady—I don't want you to misinterpret this advice as me trying to brush all your emotions under a rug. Absolutely not. What I want is for you to know that you are allowed to smile.

He will once again fill your mouth with laughter
and your lips with shouts of joy.

Job 8:21 NLT

Soul Work

Research supports the old adage that laughter is the best medicine. Interestingly, the therapeutic value of laughter is based not on just spontaneous laughter but forced laughter as well.[3] So if you can't find it spontaneously, I want you to force yourself to laugh. Take one of my suggestions or one of your own and make plans for an hour or so of light-hearted activity. Put a reminder in your calendar. Invite a friend or your spouse to join you.

Prayer Time

Lord, please replenish my heart with joy and laughter and help me accept those emotions. Amen.

Wonderfully and Fearfully Made: The Wording of Pregnancy Loss

S o you had yourself a little miscarriage" were the first words out of my Nana's mouth. Her sapphire eyes whispered sincere sympathy, but her words pierced me.

Words have a way of halting our hearts. We all know the words *miscarriage* and *stillbirth* don't adequately portray the big, huge, momentous significance of our precious child dying in our bodies. You and I both know that the loss of our babies is not insignificant or little. It's weighty. As if it could swallow us whole. Some days we wish it would just go ahead and swallow us.

The word *miscarriage* is such a misnomer, isn't it? The prefix alone goes with words such as *mistake, misspoke, mislead*. It's such a terrible prefix to attach to such a significant event. It implies we are at fault although we aren't. The word *stillbirth* isn't better. Neither are *pregnancy loss* or *born sleeping*.

Tara said, "To me the 'fetal tissue,' as my three children were being referred to, was babies, toddlers, teenagers, and adults in my mind. From the moment I found out I was pregnant, I was smitten. I pictured my life and their lives."

Truly, would any word adequately sum up such complex emotions? I struggle while writing this book. Do I say "the baby you lost" (again, it implies guilt), or use terminology such as "miscarriage"? I've yet to find a sensitive word or phrase that describes what happened when our precious baby died inside our bodies, so I use the commonly used terms. But I also use the term *death* because it speaks truth into the situation.

Do you have trouble even saying the words aloud?

You should also know that medical books and insurance paperwork call anything that happens pre-twenty weeks a *spontaneous abortion*, and at first (and second glance), this might take your breath away. Cayci recalls being at her doctor appointment following her D&C. She said she was looking at the screen while the nurse was updating her information. She was appalled to see the word *abortion*. "I could feel so many emotions racing. I was so angry. I did not abort my baby! I would do anything to have it back."

If we break down the word *spontaneous abortion*, it literally means your baby was spontaneously expelled from your body. It doesn't imply that you chose for your baby to die; it means your body expelled what was biologically unable to survive. These are clinical and medical words. And if you had to have assistance with your child departing your body—a child that was unable to survive, please know you didn't choose for this to occur. In these cases, the word *abortion* is used merely to mean a *leaving*, not a *choice*.

Don't let these misguided words define you. Each of you labored. You might have delivered your baby while sitting on the toilet, while crouched in a bathtub, while under the scalpel, or on the delivery table. The soul of your baby had already gone off to heaven, but you delivered the earthly remains from your body. Many of you felt contractions, some of you had to have surgery, and others of you were told to go home and wait for the baby to naturally come out of your body. We each birthed a baby.

Just think, when your child was in your body, the physician said, "The heart rate of your baby is …" When you had an ultrasound, the tech said, "Look at your baby kicking." And when you saw those two lines on the pregnancy test, you declared, "We are having a baby."

A loved baby took root in your womb and now blooms in heaven.

The Bible clearly states that our babes were made in secret and skillfully wrought. Life begins at conception. God is the maker. The Bible says, "You watched me as I was being formed in utter seclusion, as

I was woven together in the dark of the womb" (Psalm 139:15 NLT). Some of you snuggled this precious child, some of you swaddled your babe with a blanket, while others of you were unable to capture any part—although your heart was deeply connected to this soul.

Beloved, don't allow the words *fetus, tissue, miscarriage, stillbirth,* and *spontaneous abortion* to define the death of your child. Physicians are not poets; they are clinicians and often use clinical language. God called your child wonderfully and fearfully made. Listen to those words.

The wording of pregnancy loss compounds your already-complex emotions, but know that when it comes to words, you should focus on the ones sent to you by God, not by man.

I praise you because I am fearfully and wonderfully made.

Psalm 139:14

Soul Work

It's hard to grapple with words. Today I want you to say aloud, "My baby died in my womb" and "Our pregnancy ended too soon." Sometimes we must practice saying in private what we are eventually comfortable saying in public.

Prayer Time

Lord, it is so hard to hear the harsh words of pregnancy loss. But I know you made my child. Help me find the courage to hear these words and realize the words do not define my loss. Amen.

Words Do Hurt

H ave you walked into a funeral home to show your condolences? Your palms sweat as you stand in line. Your face blushes as you move closer and closer through the receiving line. "I'm sorry" seems too brief, but anything more edges into that murky area of further awkwardness.

I've been there too—deep in that place of nervous sympathy. Where we have no idea how to articulate sorrow.

My mother-in-law gave birth to five children, but two of her beloveds died in automobile accidents. Jesse died at the age of two and lovely Lauren died at the age of twenty. Their deaths make people uneasy. She wants to talk about the wonderful memories, but many people treat her as if her deceased children never existed. She says, "People are extremely uncomfortable talking about death and have told me over the years, 'Well, at least you have another.' As if one child could replace another."

The words of the reckless pierce like swords,
but the tongue of the wise brings healing.

Proverbs 12:18

Few of us are comfortable talking about death in *any* circumstance. And what nervously spews from our mouths often ends up being reckless, hurtful phrases. I'm sure you, in the past, have made reckless slips of the tongue too.

Pregnancy loss is especially difficult to discuss. It is a socially negated loss and in the past has been a taboo topic. It's invisible and can be challenging to resolve. Our society doesn't know how to comfort a grieving mama. I've found that reckless words, in the specific case of pregnancy loss, are often the result of misinformation on the part of the speaker, true spite, people intentionally or unintentionally minimizing our loss, and people not knowing what to say and, therefore, accidentally uttering something hurtful.

Let's explore some of the comments that grate. We've all been victim to phrases that evoke pain. Words have flogged and bruised *all* our hearts. It doesn't make it easier, but I do want to let you know that it is not just *your* friends and family that can be insensitive. You are not alone.

When Words Cast Blame

Did you know that many wrongly believe pregnancy loss can be prevented? But as I discussed earlier, loss is not the result of heavy lifting, stress, or even having sex while pregnant.[1] These false assumptions make it appear we could have *prevented* our pregnancy loss. So people wrongly tell us what we could have *done* differently.

Pregnancy loss is often the cause of a chromosomal abnormality, not something such as exercising. A misinformed person actually told our Loved Baby sister, Amanda, an avid runner, "All that running might have caused the miscarriage."

It's a bit ridiculous, isn't it? Has someone uttered a foolish phrase to you?

Georganna, an MD, recounts when she and her husband moved to a new city to begin residency. They quickly learned their new home was infested with spiders, and they had it professionally sprayed. Around this time she experienced a miscarriage. A few colleagues offered condolences when she returned to residency. But then one of the them made a piercing accusation. He said, "Oh, I bet you lost the baby because of all that spraying for spiders you did."

Can you imagine hearing those words? My heart aches for Georganna.

The false assumption that pregnancy loss is the effect of a specific action causes many people to utter comments that place *us* at blame.

In their minds, they think finding a *cause* will help our hearts. But it does the opposite. It makes us feel guilty. Dear mama, the public is vastly ignorant about the subject of pregnancy loss. Don't listen to these pseudo-physicians.

"It Was God's Will"

Many well-meaning people offer condolences that pierce. Talor recalls a person saying, "It's probably a blessing. There is a reason some babies don't make it."

Ouch. That hurts! Saying death is a reason for celebration will not help anyone. Many minimize our loss by saying phrases such as "It happened for a reason" or "It was God's will." Mia makes the claim, "I feel too often in the Christian community people want to brush over miscarriage like it's no big deal, saying things like 'You'll have another baby' or 'This was the Lord's plan for your life' without really considering what the mama is going through."

Zoe supports this comment, saying, "It was especially hurtful when people told me it was for the best and maybe I should have only one child. Those comments would make me blame myself and feel guilty for wanting another child."

Comments like these hurt big time, don't they? They make us feel as if our grief is imagined. Or that we wouldn't have cherished a baby who might have had special needs.

Tara says, "I wanted to shake some folks. One person told me, 'At least you have your other baby.' But from the minute the test said pregnant, I was attached, and red, yellow, black, blue, challenged, whatever, I love each of my children and wish they were here."

Even though we know God has a plan for our lives, at this moment in time, we are mourning the specific future we had imagined with our child. A pat response doesn't help wounded souls. Healing is dependent on doctors, caregivers, and loved ones recognizing that pregnancy loss is a death and not minimizing the event. Minimizing halts recovery. I agree with Talor's wise words, "When in doubt, just offer a hug."

"Just Adopt"

Has anyone told you to "just adopt"? Tara said of this common phrase, "We know we can adopt. We might one day, but I'm grieving the loss of a *specific baby*. One that I just lost."

Adoption is a choice that arrives after much prayer. Adoption is not a *just* situation. Not everyone has the financial ability to adopt or feels the call to this special path of motherhood. Plus, right now we are grieving a specific pain. We need support that will help us process our present reality, not plan our future.

Silence

It can be dreadful when words aren't spoken. It adds to our desolation. Kim, whose baby boy was born still at seven months, said, "It hurt when no one would ask or talk about it." As if the baby never even had an existence.

Holly says her surprise pregnancy was not well received by her family—including her spouse. Holly could easily support another baby; however, everyone thought the ones she had were enough. Her family barely acknowledged her pregnancy, and she found herself completely isolated after she had a miscarriage. She recalls that she was the only one ever emotionally invested in her child. The day following her D&C was one of the hardest of her life. Her family carried on with life as normal. "As a mom, I was grieving the thought of having my third child. It took me a long time to get past the resentment. I fully relied on God during this period."

"At Least It Happened Early"

Another caustic comment is when people put a gestational age on grief. The Bible is clear that life begins at conception. No matter the gestational age, we are mourning the loss of a child that God allowed to be conceived. Our community of Christ puts much value on the life of a baby aborted by choice. *That child could have been a doctor! Every life counts. Life begins at conception.* However, when our baby fails to progress, the loss is somehow dismissed as if it is unworthy or something we should quickly get over. This paradox makes us confused.

Attachment can begin the moment we find we have life within our wombs.

"You Can Always Have Another Baby"

This comment fails to recognize that we mourn a specific soul. It also implies it is simple to get pregnant and we will automatically have *better luck* next time. Many don't realize the private emotional and financial struggles we endure. We might have spent several attempts at IVF or spent years charting our cycles. In fact, the baby we lost might have been the light at the end of a five-year battle with infertility.

Irving Leon, a psychologist who specializes in reproductive loss, tells us, "The physical gestation might have been eight weeks at the time of the miscarriage, but if a couple struggled to get pregnant, the psychological gestation could have been eight years."[2]

Many women have pregnancies that threaten their lives. Hemorrhaging is deadly. Women have life-threatening infections. Because of this trauma, you and your spouse might decide to halt future pregnancy attempts.

Or you might be a precious soul who can no longer bear children due to a hysterectomy, a damaged fallopian tube, or other medical reasons. Jenny, an RN, had to have an emergency hysterectomy following her last loss. She still grieves the death of her uterus. Her youthful age deceives those who think she is still ripe in the middle of her childbearing years. She says, "All I ever wanted to be was a mommy, and a mommy to a house full of kids. That being said, people tell me all the time, 'Be thankful for the ones you have!' And I am. But who are they to say that to me? It's viscerally painful to know that I would have five children had they all lived. I didn't have the options of trying again after Ben was born."

Many families can't just go on to "have another baby," and it stings when people assume otherwise.

"It Happens So Often"

Holly says her mother shrugged off her loss, saying, "Well, it just happens so often." Holly told me, "Yes, it is statistically probable, but it's also common for a parent to die. But I'm not going to go to a funeral home and tell my friend, 'I'm sorry for the death of your mother. But you know…it just happens so often!'" Statistics alone do little to comfort, don't they?

Guard Your Heart

What could you add to the list? Did you want to punch the offender? Or run out of the room crying?

Beloved, we must guard ourselves from allowing the weed of bitterness to overtake our souls. Emily, a certified public accountant, says, "It hurt when people reacted like I'd lost a puppy. And followed it up by saying I could have another. I wanted the one I lost. I feel like people who haven't experienced loss unknowingly trivialize it to a degree because we never physically meet our babies. It made me mad, and still does, but I try to remind myself that I can't blame people for their reactions if they have never experienced the loss."

Emily's statement is full of truth. The people who have made these reckless comments have most likely not experienced this type of grief. It's hard to talk about or empathize with what you don't understand.

We shouldn't rely on other people to provide comfort. God is the sole source of true comfort. Being maddened with other people for their insensitive comments is a normal reaction, but we must guard ourselves from becoming bitter and furthering our pain.

People are not perfect; they *will* utter reckless comments. Brace yourself for the inevitable. I'm so sorry to say this, but someone will say something that makes you cry. Here is some gentle advice that helped me cope. When someone says something hurtful to you, repeat the verse, "There is none righteous, no, not one" (Romans 3:10 KJV), over and over in your head to help you remember that we can't expect *everyone* to be a system of positive support. People are flawed.

Above all, don't meditate on reckless comments. At night, when you lay your head on your pillow, don't let careless words repeat in your mind. Be wise and guard your heart against untruths. You might not be able to guard your *ears*, but you can guard your *heart*. Choose to meditate on truth. Your baby was wonderfully and fearfully made.

Soul Work

- Write down every hurtful comment on a single sheet of paper. Get a marker and mark them out. Then throw out the paper.

- Now, write down every single thing someone did that showed kindness. It might be something as simple as a hug or a sympathetic glance. Meditate on these acts of love.

Prayer Time

Lord, I pray that you will protect me from brash words that hurt my heart. I also pray that you will allow me to truly forgive my offenders. I will meditate on your words instead of the words of man. Your words bring healing. Amen.

Not Planting the Seeds
of Anger and Jealousy

nger. It's an emotion we all have to sort post-loss. It seeps from our hearts and darkens our spirits.

Are you a bit surprised at the forcefulness with which it spews? Has it come to visit you? This foreign invader seeks to control our thoughts. Many women are ashamed they feel such fury.

Beloved, you are normal. You haven't morphed into a different person. Anger is a reaction to grief and will manifest itself in many ways.

I want to be very real with you for a moment. I realized the extent of my rage one dark night. I was sitting outside of Walmart while my husband ran in to get a few groceries, and I saw *her*. My blood began to boil. I burst into tears.

Have you seen *her* yet?

This time she really was as bad as it could get. She emerged from her car with a cigarette hanging from her mouth, cola perched in her hand (in my imagination it was spiked with whiskey), curse words spewing from her lips, a brood of shoeless kids traveling behind her, and a pregnant belly protruding from her body.

Oh, that pregnant belly.

Days earlier I had been told I probably would never be able to have children again, and there *she* was. All *she* needed was a plate of sushi, lunchmeat, and an uncooked hotdog, and *she* would have been the poster child for "DO NOT DO WHILE PREGNANT."

Simmer down, I told myself. *Do not despise anyone*, I was reminded from a recent sermon. *Everyone is a child of God.*

But my inner dialogue kept talking.

Really? If children are a blessing from God, why is this lady not treating them as blessings?

My heart started palpitating, and I was ready to call child protective services. Did she not realize she had four precious gifts, and her job was to keep those little ones safe? *Why, God?* I asked as tears poured down my face. *Why did that mom get four kids, and you just took two from me? I did everything right. I gave up caffeine, ate all my vegetables, took my prenatal vitamins, and drank lots of water.*

My husband found me crying. He had to scoop me up and console me.

You've been there too. Haven't you?

We might be angry and stay angry for months.

Our anger is toward the negligent moms and the pregnant women who are always complaining about their pregnancies. And the women complaining about their children. We are angry at the ladies blissfully planning the month of their conceptions—so as not to interfere with work demands, a particular season, or vacation—not realizing that sometimes desires can't be planned.

We are angry at the people at our church who constantly ask when we are going to have a baby. We are angry at the people on social media announcing their pregnancies, showcasing gender reveal parties, and bragging about ultrasound pictures.

Oh anger, you tricky monster—you crawl into our hearts and make us have to battle the feelings of jealousy. It is just awful to be jealous of a woman who is pregnant.

Anger is a common thread among women who have experienced loss. In earlier devotions, we explored being angry at our bodies, being angry at others for hurting us with their words, and being angry with God. But other triggers dredge this emotion—most of all seeing other pregnant women. Lake says, "I had a hard time hearing others were pregnant. I wanted to be genuinely happy, but it was hard."

Have you had a hard time being happy for others? "Wanting that big belly for myself," as Zoe told me.

Some of us have to learn to forgive very early. It might be unavoidable at our place of work. Dana told me, "The week I returned to work after my first miscarriage, the teacher two doors down who was also pregnant posted a huge graph in the hall, where her students guessed if she was having a boy or a girl. Then a couple days after that, she posted a sign in the hall saying, 'It's a girl!' The journey to forgiveness was a long one."

Our sweet Rachel, who gave birth to twins at nineteen weeks, says, "I had a very difficult time seeing pregnant women after my miscarriage. My very good friend had twins prior to my miscarriage, and I couldn't stand to look at her. Going back to work was difficult for me as well, especially since I was starting a new job in labor delivery/nursery. I cried every time we had a delivery. I couldn't stand to see anyone that was pregnant, even if I didn't know them."

So how do we uproot this anger?

Hours after my miscarriage had been confirmed, my husband and I were sitting around the dinner table, trying to regain some sense of normalcy. I was stabbing the meatloaf on my plate. Not eating; just moving and moving it around. A car door slammed. I peered through the curtains and saw our preacher and one of the deacons ambling along our sidewalk. Neither had ever visited our house before. I assumed they were coming to offer condolences, but I wasn't sure how they'd found out the news.

My husband invited them to gather with us around the table. Southern hospitality took a backseat to my grief. I didn't even offer them sweet tea. I felt like a child, slumped in a chair, trying to be brave but really just wanting to be invisible.

Small talk. Banter. I didn't say a word. My husband carried the conversation.

Then our deacon, whom I absolutely adore, said he had some top-secret good news that he just couldn't contain. "I'm going to be having two more grandkids!" He explained that two of his children—both of which were our friends—were expecting. It turned out that the babies were due within days of the child that had just died in my body.

I closed my eyes, and the breath left my body.

I seethe. I'm livid I'm not the one announcing my news. *I'm jealous.* These two families are pregnant. *I'm ashamed.* How horrible that my first reaction to hearing this joyous news is not happiness but instead pure bitterness. *I'm confused.* Why can't I speak my pain and ask for prayer? I don't have the courage to tell them I had a miscarriage that day—I'm too ashamed. *I'm afraid.* Lord, will you take these two precious children too?

Nausea overwhelmed my body.

I started uttering a silent prayer to God. I pleaded with him to watch over those two babies. It took me corralling every negative emotion, but I was able to turn my anger into an opportunity for prayer. I prayed for those babies for seven straight months. Hard. Every time I saw the mothers, my eyes would fill with tears, but on I prayed. When it hurt, I prayed.

Do not be anxious about anything, but in every situation, by prayer and petition, with thanksgiving, present your requests to God. And the peace of God, which transcends all understanding, will guard your hearts and your minds in Christ Jesus.
Philippians 4:6–7

Now, when I see the deacon's grandchildren, I am reminded that my baby would have been their age, but I'm surrounded by peacefulness knowing I prayed without ceasing for these two joys.

Prayer didn't take away my sadness, but it did give me something constructive to do with my emotions. Prayer is our weapon when we are angry.

Has social media been a trigger for you? It can be destructive to your soul right now. You might take a fast from social media. Please don't feel guilty for taking this step toward self-preservation.

I also want you to think about something. It is statistically probable that these women who are pregnant have silently endured pregnancy loss or infertility. Let's try to convince our hearts to cheer on and encourage our sweet sisters instead of filling our minds with anger. We might not have the strength to be in the same room with them right now, but we can pray for them. I'm not saying it's easy, but prayer can ease the hurt.

Soul Work

- Perhaps you are now watching a friend go through her pregnancy. Commit to praying for this mama when grief overwhelms your soul.

- Has social media been destructive or constructive for your healing? Take a break if you need.

Prayer Time

Lord, this jealousy and anger hold me captive. I don't want to be a jealous person. You instruct us to combat our anxiety with prayer. Lord, I know you are available for me to talk to you whenever I feel these negative emotions stirring in my soul. Amen.

Born into the Splendor of Heaven

*L*ast night I wandered around our vineyard on the east side of our home, eating the last of the muscadines. A bit of sweetness plucked straight from the vine. The time has changed, and day turned to night a bit swiftly. But it gave me an opportunity to gaze above my head. The big, black, vast expanse was bathed in twinkling lights and a crescent moon.

Can you imagine the questions our ancestors had about this mysterious majesty that blankets our world each night? It made me start thinking about things above. Those questions about heaven and our babes.

After I found out that my babes had died in my womb, theological questions swirled in my mind. *Did this child have a soul? Would I have the opportunity to see my child in heaven?*

So I started searching. I needed answers. Not those quick, easy answers people write on the bottom of a sympathy card or whisper in our ear, telling us that so-and-so is in a better place. Those answers fall flat. I wanted answers that come after searching and combing over the Scriptures and through books by the great theologians.

I dug deep. And I want to share the harvest of my toil with you. Because the answers can bring such absolute comfort on days when you feel as if you might go crazy. I want you to lean in as I share something with you as brilliant as the stars above.

The babies that died in our wombs were born
straight into the splendor of heaven.

Our babies are dancing on streets of gold (Revelation 21:21) within those pearly gates (Revelation 21:21). They are filling up our mansions (John 14:2) and eating from the great vineyard (Isaiah 65:21). They are living a life of eternal pleasure (Psalm 16:11) with other believers.

Doesn't that sound wonderful? This is where our children are right now. And I know it doesn't eradicate the pain of the now, but I need you to dig your roots deep in this hope and promise. Let's take a look at the Scriptures.

Your Child Is a Life

The Bible assures us that every single life conceived is a precious, God-ordained life. Psalm 139:13–15 beautifully describes life being knit together in the mother's womb. The psalmist also says, "From my mother's womb you have been my God" (Psalm 22:10).

This tells us that every single life conceived is a person. Whether your child died at four weeks old or forty weeks old, your baby is a life, created by God.

Your Child Is in Heaven

These precious souls that God knit into our wombs do not cease to exist, rather they all exist in heaven. The apostle Paul writes, "We are confident, I say, and would prefer to be away from the body and at home with the Lord" (2 Corinthians 5:8).

Did you catch that? To be away from the body means to be at home with the Lord. Isn't that a wonderful word? *Home.* Our children are at home. The place where we yearn to be. It's a reminder that the life we currently live is temporal, while our future life is eternal.

Your Child Is Saved by God's Mercy

Our God is merciful. Our babes are innocents. They didn't know sin. God accepted the hearts of the children that died in our wombs into his kingdom without a second glance.

How do I know this? The Bible tells me so in explicit terms. So explicit that I was left absolutely breathless one morning as I was poring over the book of Job with a cup of coffee.

Heaven is described for a stillborn child.

Yes, you read that correctly. God's Word mentions our children who died in our wombs in his book. The Bible depicts life for our children that died in the womb as perfect.

Listen to what Job—who was in absolute misery—says:

Why did I not perish at birth,
and die as I came from the womb?
Why were there knees to receive me
and breasts that I might be nursed?
For now I would be lying down in peace;
I would be asleep and at rest
with kings and rulers of the earth,
who built for themselves places now lying in ruins,
with princes who had gold,
who filled their houses with silver.
Or why was I not hidden away in the ground like a stillborn child,
like an infant who never saw the light of day?
There the wicked cease from turmoil,
and there the weary are at rest.
Captives also enjoy their ease;
they no longer hear the slave driver's shout.
The small and the great are there,
and the slaves are freed from their owners. (Job 3:11–19)

Job describes heaven in perfect terms for a stillborn child. It is a place of peace, rest, and ease. It is a place where we will be surrounded by other believers.

My mother delivered a perfectly formed little boy with a head full of black hair at seven months. She was so thankful to get to hold him and kiss him. An autopsy showed no known reason for premature birth. My father had a private burial for him while my mother was in the hospital.

I can't even imagine the pain that she and so many of you have felt with a late-term loss. But she rests knowing that although his body is in the church graveyard, his soul is in heaven with God.

Our babies had automatic adoption into the kingdom of heaven. These children of ours never have to toil or tarry. As parents we never have to worry about their souls, or their feelings getting hurt, or broken legs, or broken anything. Our treasure is in heaven. Although this is supremely challenging, instead of thinking of God as mean, we should try to recognize God as merciful to our child conceived. Our children now have a life without pain, without discord. A life of pure joy.

I remain confident of this:
I will see the goodness of the LORD
in the land of the living.

Psalm 27:13

Say that Scripture aloud. Now replace the word *goodness* with the name of your child or the word *baby*.

You Will See Your Child Again

Sweet mama, our sanity rests on the premise that our life with this little one is not one of a true goodbye. We have the opportunity to embrace our child again in heaven. And just as God promises that life in heaven will be bliss, he also warned us that life on earth will be burdensome and we will have a longing that can't be quenched. "For while we are in this tent, *we groan and are burdened*, because we do not wish to be unclothed but to be *clothed instead with our heavenly dwelling*, so that what is mortal may be swallowed up by life. Now the one who has fashioned us for this very purpose is God, who has given us the Spirit as a deposit, guaranteeing what is to come" (2 Corinthians 5:4–5).

I realize your heart is aching to the point that you are only living in the now, and you can't live in the future promises. I get it. But I'm trying to slowly fill your cup with promises from God, so these promises can percolate and slowly drip into the empty cavern in your soul, until one day they build to a fullness of belief that your child is in a truly better place. A place where we have the opportunity of gaining entry. God has given us the Spirit as a deposit.

Heaven is a majestic place. We can remain confident that although we are hurting, our child is not. And wouldn't any one of us make that sacrifice for any of our children? Wouldn't any of us bear pain so they bear none?

You are bearing that pain right now, dear one. But know that one day you too will dance, twist, and shout on the same streets of gold that your little one is now skipping across.

Soul Work

- Reread Job 3:11–19. Underline all the words that describe heaven.

- It can be helpful to visualize your child in heaven. Who is there with your child? Write a letter to them asking them to watch over your little one.

Prayer Time

Lord, I pray for peace to fill my soul,
for I know my child is in heaven. Amen.

Ectopic Pregnancy

$\mathcal{E}$ malee didn't know she was pregnant when the severe, labor-like pain began. She rushed to the hospital, where she found she had active internal bleeding due to a burst fallopian tube. Her life was at risk. Diagnosis: ectopic pregnancy. The doctor had no explanation for why she wasn't already dead from the amount of blood seeping from her body. "God isn't ready for you," he told her as he took her in for emergency surgery.

The pain wasn't just physical but also full of emotional and spiritual toil. She struggled with what medically had to be done. Emalee said, "As an animal scientist, my head was saying, 'Biologically this baby is not viable and cannot develop in my tube.' My head was also saying, 'My own life is in danger, and I have a twelve-month-old who needs her mama.' My heart as a Christian was saying otherwise. It was tough. My husband helped me through it by reminding me that the baby had no heartbeat, that he and our daughter needed us, and that God had other plans for me. My left tube was removed in the process, but three months later I became pregnant (by surprise) with our second child, who is now fourteen months old."

About 2 percent of pregnancies are ectopic.[1] The March of Dimes reminds us that an ectopic pregnancy cannot grow to produce a healthy baby. Ectopic literally means "out of place," because the fertilized egg is growing outside the uterus. Ectopic pregnancies occur most often in the fallopian tube. Without treatment (surgery or medicine to stop the growth of the embryo), the pregnancy will continue to grow and the fallopian tube will burst. Then life-threatening internal bleeding will occur. About 1 in 50 pregnancies in the United States are ectopic.[2]

But ectopic pregnancy goes beyond this medical trauma, doesn't it? It is a tender turmoil.

Your Extra Fears Are Normal

You are not only mourning the loss of your child, but you had fears you would die. Now you have increased fears as to whether or not you will be able to have additional children and if *this* will happen again. It is so much to wrap your mind around, isn't it? Where do you even begin to heal when wounds have been pierced in so many places?

Having one ectopic pregnancy does put you at an increased risk for another. But please keep reading—as there is hope.

The March of Dimes reports, "If you've had an ectopic pregnancy, you have about a 3 in 20 chance (15 percent) of having another."[3] Look again at that statistic. You are more likely to have a healthy pregnancy than to have another ectopic pregnancy. There is hope.

In addition to mourning the loss of your baby, you and your husband also have to decide whether or not you want to try to conceive again. Don't rush this decision or conversation. Distance yourself a bit from the grief before you make any definitive answers. Know that this can be a challenging decision because your life was at risk. Many women report their husbands are hesitant. Some partners even refuse. Please try to understand their perspective and give them time. They experienced the loss of their baby, and they also faced the potential loss of you. Also know that your response and your husband's to trying again will be reactionary. Both of your minds might change after you have a bit of space from the current trauma.

Be willing to talk to your partner and acknowledge their fears as well as yours. Don't push your husband away if he isn't quite ready to try again. Refuse to allow this to become a wedge in your marriage. Give it some time, and if the discussion is still difficult, consider talking to your pastor, a counselor, or your healthcare provider.

Dear heart, don't feel abnormal if you or your partner have these extra concerns. It's only natural, isn't it? Seek out a friend who can offer support by listening to your fears, journal your thoughts, or join a support group so you can connect with women who've had similar experiences.

You Did Not Have an Elective Abortion

After any type of loss, we all have whispers of guilt that enter our consciousness. But you have an extra layer of questions. You may have discovered that your baby was in your tube before a rupture occurred. Your baby couldn't survive in the environment outside your womb. Allowing the baby to continue to grow would have been life-threatening for you. You had to take one of two paths: surgery or medicine.

Some women have wrestled with the question of whether this treatment of ectopic pregnancy is elective abortion. You did not *elect* for your child to grow in an environment where it could not survive, and you did not *elect* for your baby to grow in an environment where rupture would occur and could lead to your own death. Therefore, you did not elect or ever wish to terminate your baby.

Do not allow the words of ignorant individuals to shame you. I pace with madness at commentaries on the Internet and uninformed words my friends have heard. The words of the reckless truly pierce like swords. Put your trust in the words of wise and thoughtful individuals.

The American Association of Pro-Life Obstetricians has a statement regarding treatment of ectopic pregnancy:

> In either case, the intent for the pro-life physician is not to kill the unborn child, but to preserve the life of the mother in a situation where the life of the child cannot be saved by current medical technology. For these reasons the American Association of Pro-Life Obstetricians recognizes the unavoidable loss of human life that occurs in an ectopic pregnancy, but does not consider treatment of ectopic pregnancy by standard surgical or medical procedures to be the moral equivalent of elective abortion, or to be the wrongful taking of human life.[4]

Find peace in those words. Meditate on them and don't rely on opinions from individuals who are ignorant of the situation. Do expect that some people might utter insensitive comments. This is unfortunate.

Our sweet Loved Baby sister Jessica had an ectopic pregnancy, and her fallopian tube ruptured. She says, "When they realize the pregnancy is ectopic, you basically have to choose to terminate. As a Christian, this bothered me on numerous levels, but my baby did not have a heartbeat and could not live without my body. I was sharing my struggle in Sunday school and trying to explain how I couldn't understand how people abort. After hearing I had to terminate, my teacher looked at me and said, 'And you're okay with that?' I was so angry. I found him after church and told him he was going to understand what I did and why I did it."

Many of you might have a situation or conversation like Jessica's. Please do not take their words to heart. Do not rely on the words of the reckless.

It's hard, sweet one. Guard your heart by sharing your soul story with people who are supportive.

You Should Receive Extra Care

If you conceive again, you should expect (and demand) extra care. Because you have an increased risk of having another ectopic pregnancy, your physician will begin monitoring your HCG level as soon as you see a positive on a home pregnancy test. Then, around six weeks, you should have an ultrasound to detect whether or not the gestational sac is in the uterus.

We are advocates of our own health. If, at any point, you feel as if your caretaker is not using proper protocol, please know it is your right to seek out another physician. Don't ignore your symptoms.

As an ectopic mother, you are mourning the loss of a baby. Many of you are also mourning the loss of a body part that helps our bodies conceive. And you were faced with your own mortality. It's a deep, dark well of a place.

Darling, I can't answer *why* God allowed this to happen or why other terrible things occur in life. But I do know that God has plans for you on this earth right now. Anchor your soul in the word of God.

We have this hope as an anchor for the soul, firm and secure.
Hebrews 6:19

Beloved, please hear this prayer written especially for you by a pastor:

This broken world in which we live has dealt you cruelty. All I can effectively do is lift you, your spirit, your situation, your family, and your future to a heavenly Father who knows your heart and feels your pain. You may not appreciate that thought right now. You may even be angry at a God who allowed this to happen. That's okay, he knows that too.

When you cry out, "Why did this happen?" or "How could this happen?" may you find the presence and comfort of a God who cares and understands.

When you feel guilt and pain, may you find the presence and comfort of a God who cares and understands. When you feel the real or perceived judgment and misunderstanding of others, may you find the presence and comfort of a God who cares and understands. May you also be blessed with the comfort of wise, patient, godly friends who know when to speak and when to be silent so that amid great grief and sorrow, you may find comfort for today and tomorrow.

"Grace and peace be yours in abundance through the knowledge of God and of Jesus our Lord." (2 Peter 1:2)

Amen.

—Randy Harmon

When Your Mind and Body Remind You of Your Loss

Sweet mamas, it is a quandary. On one hand, we want to be reminded of our baby, but on the other, we don't want reminders that magnify the ache.

In the very early days, it is often our bodies that remind us of the moment of loss. Most mamas feel drained both physically and mentally. Our minds and bodies go through trauma, and, unfortunately, as time progresses reminders will continue.

Let's explore some issues you might face in the days and months ahead.

Breasts

Has your milk come in? Do you wonder what to do to stop the pain of engorgement? Some women donate their milk to a milk bank. However, most use methods to stop the production. Many recommend using ice packs or chilled or room temperature green cabbage leaves to help relieve engorgement. A warm shower can also help you release a bit of milk. Expressing a little milk—just enough to relieve the fullness, even if it is only a few drops—can also help you feel more comfortable. This will not increase milk supply but might help prevent complications like mastitis.

Contact the lactation consultant at the hospital where you delivered or call the office of your healthcare provider and ask to speak to a consultant. They can give you much-needed support.

Bleeding

Whether you've had an early or a late-term pregnancy loss, you will have bleeding. The timing will depend upon your type of loss and your own particular body. You do need to call your healthcare provider if you are saturating more than two pads per hour, have severe pain, or have fever or chills.[1] These can be signs of infection. Do not be alarmed if you see clots for some days following your loss. Don't hesitate to consult your healthcare provider if you have any questions.

Menstruation

Your period could return within four to six weeks. However, you can ovulate and become pregnant as soon as two weeks after an early miscarriage.[2] Many women are comforted by the arrival of their period, because it means their bodies are functioning properly and they can begin the process of conceiving again. But other women are greatly distressed by the arrival of their period, as it is a visual reminder of loss and a reminder that they are not pregnant. If you had a traumatic delivery, it can be especially troublesome. It will get easier, but initially it is challenging to see this trigger. As always, call your physician if you are worried about your period.

Weight

Kim says it was so hard "to lose that baby weight gain with no baby to hold." Our extra body weight after loss makes many of us angry, and it's hard when maternity clothes still have to be worn. Ask your doctor when you can resume exercise. Eat healthy, but try not to focus on the number on your scale. Exercising and making good food choices will boost your emotional spirit. If your budget allows, you might also go ahead and purchase a few non-maternity clothing items in your current size. Fresh clothing will help boost your spirit and begin helping you separate your identity as a pregnant woman.

Night Terrors

Restless sleep is a common side effect of pregnancy loss. Almost half of the women in a research study experienced nightmares post-loss and these often included visions of their baby and blood.[3] Some good sleep habits are: reading or listening to soothing music before bedtime, drinking herbal tea, taking a shower or bubble bath with lavender, choosing an affirmation or Scripture to repeat when you awaken, and diffusing essential oils. If you continue to have restless sleep, you might consider talking to your physician about whether or not you should try sleeping medication. Try to avoid having screen time before bed. I know these sound like rather easy solutions to a very complicated problem. None of these are magic elixirs, but they might help bring you a bit of peace.

Bereavement Leave

If your job offers bereavement leave, you might consider taking it in addition to your sick leave. You might also investigate taking a longer leave. Call your human resources department, ask a manager, or talk to your physician for advice.

Mail

Expect to receive promotions for formula, baby magazines, or coupons for baby stores. It's a struggle to see these items. Please consider having someone take over mail duty for a few months. Ask your husband to check the mailbox and discard these items.

E-mail

Ask someone to go through your e-mail to unsubscribe you from sites such as Baby Center and other pregnancy apps. Some of these sites we never even opted into, but they find us. The unroll.me app can help you unsubscribe from unwelcome e-mail. If you get unwelcome mail in your inbox, mark it as junk mail and block it, or scroll to the bottom of the e-mail and click "unsubscribe;" otherwise, they will keep coming.

Social Media

The ability to connect with others via social media is wonderful and yet horrible. It is difficult to turn on social media and see pregnancy announcements, bump updates, and families with their babies.

Tara says, "I would see post after post on Facebook of people being pregnant, and each time I'd cry." These triggers can cause emotional distress. Take care of yourself. Take a social media fast and focus on real relationships by texting, phone calls, and person-to-person visits. But if you find social media enjoyable, you might consider "unfollowing" certain friends. Doing this means you will continue being "friends," but you won't see their posts in your newsfeed. You can also do the same for Instagram, Twitter, and other applications you might use. Facebook even has app features such as groups. This can be downloaded, so you can stay a member of groups, such as pregnancy loss support groups, without having to scroll through the main screen of Facebook.

What if you've announced your pregnancy on social media? Do you deliver a statement that your baby passed away? This is also your call depending on your grieving style. Many women report that it helps to make a statement as support rushes in from all sides. Should you share photos of your little love? Many women prefer to keep these private, so they can't be shared, while others find comfort in sharing their baby with their friends. There is no easy answer. You could start out by sharing in a pregnancy loss support group and then sharing with your family and friends. Commemorative photos are beautiful and do allow others to share in your mourning. Talk it over with your spouse and trust your decision.

Nursery

The quiet void of a decorated nursery is haunting. Don't rush into plans of taking down the room or moving furniture. Take time to decide what you'll do with the room and the contents. Perhaps you can choose a future month as a time when you will make a decision. When that month arrives, you can begin evaluating what you are going to do with the contents. Inviting a trusted friend or family member into the process might be helpful. Redecorating the room will be challenging because it is a concrete dismantling of the dreams you had for you and your child. Take a photograph of the room and the contents—that way you can add the pictures to this commemorative book.

Items Bought

You've purchased maternity wear, baby clothing, bibs, and bottles. You might have books and blankets intended for your child. Keep a special drawer for selected items you've purchased. Or donate the items to a family in need. You know what will bring your heart the most peace. Don't let anyone make this decision for you—trust your instincts. If it is hard letting go, you can have a blanket made of the items or take pictures of the items before you release them.

Hospital Bills

Paying the hospital and healthcare provider is especially troubling. Camila says, "The medical bills I received made me so angry! Being billed for a full delivery seemed like such a slap in the face. I get that someone has to pay for it, but I would cry my eyes out every time a new bill came." Ask your partner to handle this task so you physically don't have to see the invoices and make the payments. You can also call the hospital and ask the accounting department to give you a discount if you pay in full. This will help alleviate some financial concerns and not prolong the payment process.

Visiting the Doctor's Office Again

We have great anxiety at revisiting the place where the bad news was received. You will probably visit your healthcare provider for a follow-up in the weeks following your loss. The sounds, smell, and surroundings will trigger pain. It's also challenging to see other women who are pregnant in the building. This is a time to ask a friend or your spouse to attend the visit with you. They can offer emotional support, but they can also help keep you focused on asking questions and remembering information. Take a list of questions with you. You can also call ahead or ask the receptionist if there is a room you can sit in, so you don't have to remain in the waiting room. Explain that you've had a loss.

Invitations to Baby Showers

Camila advises, "Listen to your heart. You know yourself better than anyone, and you will know when you are ready to deal with reality. A girl I worked with was due one week before I was, and she had a baby shower two months after my stillbirth. Everyone was going. I felt selfish if I didn't go. Everyone kept telling me I didn't have to go, especially my husband, but I didn't want to act weak, and I didn't want people feeling sorry for me, so I went, and I regret it. I was fine until she started opening presents, and then I lost it. There were men there also, so thankfully my husband was in attendance. But to this day, I wish I hadn't gone. I felt like I needed to 'get over it' and move on, but I wasn't ready for that." Send a gift or a card. Know you can decline the invitation and say you already had plans. By plans you can just mean that you are planning to take care of yourself. You don't have to explain. Protect yourself. By saying no to an event such as a gender reveal or a baby shower, you are saying yes to your recovery. You'll eventually get to a place where you can celebrate, but right now it might be too much.

Soul Work

Do you have mementos of your child? Gather the ultrasound pictures and photos and any other documents and put them together. Take photos of special items you purchased or put them in a special box or drawer.

Prayer Time

Lord, as these reminders of my baby continue to emerge, please help my heart to grow stronger as I continue to ache for my child. Amen.

Inviting Others into Your Fellowship

I sent them a text message. Yes, that is how my two dearest friends discovered I was pregnant and that I was miscarrying. All in two simple sentences. "Perry is driving me the doctor. I think I'm having a miscarriage." Bless their hearts. Chrissi and Tonya, my two best friends who taught next door to one another, say they got my message, found one another, and retreated to the bathroom across the hall so they could cry and pray for me.

There is no Emily Post guideline for announcing a miscarriage or stillbirth. Yes, it did startle my friends, but in all respects, a loss is a startling event for all involved, and I don't know if a gentle way to convey the information exists.

All I know is that I needed them to be in my fellowship. I knew I would need their comfort, but saying it aloud was too painful. We all need fellowship. You might not be able to find it in person, so seek out a community online. But find souls who will commit to pray for and encourage you.

Two are better than one,
because they have a good return for their labor:
If either of them falls down,
one can help the other up.

Ecclesiastes 4:9–10

My best friends were wonderful. I asked very few people into my fellowship, but those in which I did confide delivered me love. Tonya brought boxes and boxes of Chinese food, Leighann brought a dozen hot, still-gooey, straight-out-of-the-oven cookies, Amber brought the most delectable chocolate cupcakes I have ever eaten, Chrissi brought a beautiful flower for me to plant, and Mary sent a heartfelt letter via e-mail. They dropped off their tokens of love, wrapped me in their arms while I cried and they cried, sat beside me in my grief, and then quietly exited my house.

My parents watched my son, and my brother called me daily just to say he cared.

Later on, they asked questions and allowed me to talk, but first they instinctively knew to show me quiet love.

Deciding who to confide in and how to confide in them is a decision we all must make. We need people to honor what we need.

Because my miscarriages were early, very few people knew I was pregnant. I chose to tell very few people. I needed to process my grief quietly. Some of you don't have this choice. You might have already shared your news at a family gathering or on social media. You might have been so far along that friends and strangers could see that you were pregnant.

We do need to invite a tribe into our lives. Evidence suggests that social support can be critical in mitigating the grief response following pregnancy loss.[1] We need a godly tribe who will be gentle and allow us to be vulnerable.

Do you know who you can invite into the dialogue of your soul? It's not the time to be a people pleaser, so give yourself permission to distance yourself from particular friends if you need to. Make a thoughtful decision, based upon your needs, of who you want to be around in the days that follow. Here are some guidelines to ponder:

1. Ask yourself: who do you want around you during this difficult time? Certain friends, certain family, certain circles of people? Do you want to make a public announcement on social media? Many women find comfort in this as it often provides a rally cry of support, but others are more hesitant to share in the public sphere. Trust yourself.

2. Ask yourself if there is anyone you do not want around (a talkative neighbor, insensitive friend, etc.).

3. Who do you need to contact? Do you need to take off from work? Do you want your church to pray for you? Do you need to make childcare arrangements? Do you need to make follow-up physician appointments?

4. Designate a gatekeeper. A gatekeeper is someone that is very close to you, perhaps your mom or your spouse, that can, for the immediate time afterward, try to uphold your wishes. They will only let those you want around you to be around you. They will field phone calls, texts, and visits. They might call your workplace or close friends for you. They can arrange childcare. They might call a friend to come visit you. Tell them your wishes. One of my friends called a workplace colleague and instructed her that when she returned to work she didn't want people to constantly come up to her giving her condolences. She just wanted to carry on as normal while at work.

5. Put your gatekeepers in place and rest. Please give your gatekeeper grace. They might not be able to follow your wishes, but having a plan in place to protect you at this fragile time might be helpful. Also, be open. A lady you don't know very well might enter your home bearing sympathy, because she too has faced this.

We all need a place to talk. But we have to be ready and willing to speak our pain. The lesson I've learned is that it is okay to be choosy about who we share our most sacred emotions with. Cancer. Miscarriage. Death. Divorce. Likewise, it's okay if we are vocal from day one. We are all different. And we must respect and honor our varied needs.

It's a fine line to walk. Being vulnerable and protecting our hearts. Expect some people to hurt you with their words, but know that many empathetic dears will wrap you in a warm embrace of support.

Tokens of Love Do Bring Comfort

These Loved Baby sisters shared some of the tokens of love they received when they were grieving.

TALOR: "My sister-in-law sat by my side and said she would never forget my baby. Having someone make that vow was precious to me."

CAMILA: "My husband held me while I cried. He just held me while I cried."

LYNDA: "My sister-in-law told me to name my babies."

TARA: "My mom was my rock and just let me grieve."

MIA: "My friend brought me a bouquet and told me it was okay to feel sad/angry/upset."

EMILY: "My husband took my son to buy me flowers, and my friend brought me cupcakes."

DEBRA: "My parents took our older children for a week, so I could attempt a natural miscarriage."

SHANNON: "My husband told me he would love me even if I couldn't carry a baby."

Soul Work

Have you sought fellowship? Grief makes many uncomfortable. Your friends and family don't know how to handle this any better than you do. Ask for what you need. If you feel isolated, please seek community through a support group—either in person or online. You are loved.

Prayer Time

Lord, I pray for fellowship. Send someone into my life that can help me mourn and lead me toward you. Amen.

Reconnecting with Who You Are

I swing open the back door to my friend Amber's house (the same friend who offered me her uterus) and let myself into her home. "You better not have knocked!" she yells. I didn't. I know better. She'd take it as a sign of impoliteness. I walk over the pine floors to find her in her kitchen, stirring a pot of something sweet on the stove. I'm not enough of a cook to know what goodness she had put together to make those pecan pralines, but I do know they were delicious.

"I always find you at your stove," I say, smiling. And that's the truth. It's who she is. Cooking makes her soul sing and brings her peace. She's the friend I called one night to see if she had a boxed mix to make cookies. I needed them to fulfill an obligation. She laughed. "Don't have boxed cookie mix, but I did make 110 cupcakes today. You're welcome to them."

God makes each of us unique. Different gifts. Different passions. Different stress relief gimmicks. For Amber, it's cooking. To you it might be something else.

Right now, you are at a place where your entire mind is fixated on your loss. Getting out of bed is difficult. You are mourning the loss of a precious child. You are also mourning the loss of your intended role as a mother. Taking time to grieve is valid and needed, but I want you to go ahead and start thinking about ways that you can reconnect with yourself.

Elizabeth Edwards says of her resilience after the death of her teenage son, "She stood in the storm, and when the wind did not blow her way—and it surely has not—she adjusted her sails."[1]

Sweet mama, we must adjust our sails. Many women cite that getting involved in hobbies, sports, and ministry helps them redirect their focus. We must cherish ourselves and refresh our spirits by seeking out ways to recognize who we are as God's creation—beloved, set apart for him, and made for a great number of purposes.

Changing Your Internal Dialogue

So many women (myself included) felt like a complete failure after their loss. Some of us had planned since we were children that our greatest goal in life was to be a mother—as many times as we wished. When this goal fails, we wander in a state of unease. We feel totally displaced from who we are. I felt like I was occupying the same body, but I didn't feel like the same person as I was before my baby died.

I knew I'd never have my baby back, but I desperately wanted to have the "old me" back. I wanted to smile, laugh, and feel comfortable in my own skin. Not like I was walking through a murky fog.

I finally realized that the first step toward reconnecting with myself was to brush aside the negative self-talk that was consuming my soul. The Bible states: "Guard your heart above all else, for it determines the course of your life" (Proverbs 4:23 NLT).

Since life can be shaped by our thoughts, we need to carefully choose what we are telling ourselves. I started telling myself the words Kathryn Stockett writes in her best-selling book *The Help*, "You kind. You smart. You important."[2]

We are more than mothers. We are more than wives. Our biggest role is that we are daughters of God. We are not failures but beloved creations of God, and our worth is not in how many or if we can have children. He has equipped us all with specific gifts and purposes. For the time being, mothering this child who was just born into heaven is not the plan he arranged. We must devise a way to march forward. To seek contentment in the day.

Now you are the body of Christ, and each one of you is a part of it.

1 Corinthians 12:27

Working through Your Grief

Sharron, who has experienced an ectopic pregnancy, a late-term loss, and a stillbirth, found that she literally had to sweat out her grief. She says, "As crazy as this seems, my family has a motto for grief and loss: 'Work through it.' My daddy taught me this by example. When I am physically exhausted, the heartache doesn't seem as great. Six weeks after the loss of our stillborn son, I bought a house to renovate as a rental. I ripped up floors, tore down walls, hung and finished new Sheetrock, and laid hardwood floors. It was exhausting, but working through it actually helps. I'm not sure I would recommend it to everyone, but it was good for me."

Sharron explains that finding something to divert her mind aided in her personal recovery. It helped her to take control of a project when the rest of her life was beyond her control.

Many women report similar stories. My mother says that my grandmother invited her to attend a quilting class. They had "assignments" to be finished before the meetings. My other grandmother also taught her to crochet. Between quilting and making afghans for everyone, her "thinking" time gradually became more positive because it was focused on completing a specific task. She also started working through her grief by completing tasks over which she had control.

We can all work through our grief and reconnect with ourselves in different ways. Whether this comes in the extreme form of home renovation or the quieter task of handiwork, we must each choose to engage in a few enjoyable tasks that help divert our minds from the replay that is constant.

Try new experiences.

Some women find renewal by engaging in new experiences. A common theme among women is literally that a change of view helped their spirit. If finances allow, consider getting away for a few days. Tara—who experienced three losses in addition to other family tragedies—cites that going away on a cruise with her mother was healing. Lynda went away to a family cabin in the Adirondacks to read, journal, and grieve. My best friend swept me away for a weekend girls' trip a month after my second loss. The anticipation of a trip, forcing myself to get dressed up, and just laughing helped me reconnect with myself.

Set goals.

We also need to set realistic goals. Make a list of tasks you can accomplish each day. It might begin with just a few things such as: get out of bed, make coffee, shower, put on makeup, call a friend, read for twenty minutes, etc. Put a few items on the list that help your soul breathe. If cooking is your jam, go grocery shopping and stir up a favorite recipe. If you are a runner, put on your shoes, blast that playlist, and go for a jog.

Just do something that refreshes your spirit and makes you feel like yourself. Making a list and following through can give you a small semblance of normalcy.

Give yourself permission to spend time on you.

Debra, who was having nightmares, marriage problems, and parenting problems, pleaded to God as most of us have. "When will I be normal again?" The Holy Spirit interceded, and she learned that the pain she felt was for a purpose. She realized that sometimes pain can be used to create new life—even within our own souls. Debra learned she was to take this time to work on herself, to learn from the experience, and to become a better person from the suffering.

Darling, we can't delete the pain, but we can take healthy precautions to distance ourselves from the searing voices and memories our minds want to constantly relive.

After my losses, I took to the stage of our community theater. Forcing my mind to be filled with learning page after page of dialogue provided me goals to accomplish. It also gave me a place to explore my emotions. Go ahead and ask a doctor what activities you should avoid and then go try something new or something you know you enjoy. Here are some ideas:

- Dance to music you listened to in high school or college.
- Go outside and learn about the constellations.
- Try out a new recipe.
- Work on making your home a refuge.
- Light a favorite scented candle and settle in to read a book.
- Go hiking, bike riding, or running. Maybe try skydiving!
- Plan a road trip or vacation.
- Volunteer to help. Going outside ourselves is good for our spirits.
- Get outside and plant something.

Prayer Time

Lord, you made me perfect. I am a child of God. I am made to bear fruit. I am chosen by you. Help me find my worth in you. Amen.

A Sibling in Heaven

I t is difficult to mourn and at the same time to help others in your family grieve. Is this your child's first experience with death? Is this your first time trying to explain to a child the hard concept of heaven? This makes it extra challenging.

Sharron says of coming home from the hospital and telling her daughter about the stillbirth of their son, "We tried to explain that her baby brother had gone to heaven. She became very emotional and was inconsolably crying that she wanted her brother here and not in heaven. She had prayed daily for a baby for our family. Dealing with her heartbreak made the loss even more painful. My advice is to not rush into the conversation. I told her immediately after coming home from the hospital. This was a mistake. I should have given both of us more time to prepare."

Although it's hard to prepare, there are some things we need to be careful of when talking to our child about the death of their sibling.

Tell the truth honestly and simply.

Consider the age and maturity of your child before you start speaking. During your initial conversation, tell the truth about the pregnancy loss in very simple terms.

Do you remember the Amelia Bedelia books from your youth? Amelia always got into trouble, because she took words at their literal meaning. For example, she makes a "sponge cake" out of bath sponges. Our children might do the same thing if we tell them "the baby is sleeping" or "we lost the baby." If your child has a limited view of heaven, they will ask why you can't get in the car and go there. Even if it is hard for you to utter, you should choose simple language. "The baby that was growing in my belly died. We are very sad," is actually much easier for a child to accept than, "We lost the baby."

Experts say, "Even when the truth is upsetting, talking about the truth is reassuring. What they know happened is often easier for them to handle than what they imagine happened, because it is finite and they can talk about it together with us."[1] Simple words help with misunderstandings.

Be prepared for your child to have anger at God if you say something such as, "God needed our baby." If you explain your loss in spiritual terms, you need to be prepared to have spiritual answers that bring peace and not fear. Always consider your child's age and emotional maturity as you decide what you will say.

Understand that questions will linger.

Expect your child to have a lot of questions and emotions about the disappearance of their sibling. These questions might happen immediately after you speak and might continue to unroll months and months later. Please realize that the subject of death might make your child fearful about their own mortality and your mortality as their parent. They might be so mad that they want to go to heaven too. They might also try to wish or pray the child back. Please try to offer them comfort, but give yourself grace. It's hard to usher our children into understanding what we ourselves often don't even understand. Questions you might anticipate are:

- Where did the baby go?
- Where is heaven?
- Can we pray for the baby to come back?
- What happened at the hospital?
- Why is God mean?
- Will I die?
- Will I go to heaven?
- Is there hot cocoa in heaven? Are there cars in heaven? Can we swim in heaven?

You might want to have some books about heaven available (a list is available on my website).

Allow room for expression.

Giving children room to create and draw can be helpful in knowing what is going on in their minds. Plus it gives them a way to express their emotions. While discussing the loss, you might ask your child to draw a picture of your family and add a picture of your baby in heaven. This can help them create a concrete and compassionate representation of what is in their minds. Reassure your child that one day we can visit them, but they will not be able to come back to us.

Can I bring him back again? I will go to him one day, but he cannot return to me.

2 Samuel 12:23 NLT

You will have different emotions toward your child.

In the days of fresh grief, you might find solace if your child is with you or you might find yourself growing distant from your child. You are grieving. Give yourself grace to feel what you feel. Ask for help if you need space. But also stay true to yourself if you just want to sit on the couch snuggled with your little one with a carton of ice cream and a movie.

The most important thing you can do during this time is to tell your child you love them and appreciate them. Listen and respect their need to talk, to cry, or to act like the kid they are. If you can't emotionally be this person, please allow another loved person in your child's life to shower them with support while you spend time grieving the way you need to. Please consider letting your child's teacher know of the situation, so they can be prepared for conversations or can recommend help.

If you feel overwhelmed, please reach out to a minister or counselor. They are trained to help little ones understand the concepts of death and dying.

Children also have a faith we can't imagine. When Hailee was three, she entered the hospital room of her grandmother who was scared and dying of cancer. In the boldness of a toddler and in an unexplainable moment, she declared, "Gran, be quiet and let God do his work. You won't be lonely; you'll rock my sisters."

Sweet mamas, don't bear the weight of trying to explain what is hard to describe. Call on the Holy Spirit for guidance and let him do the work. He can use this pain to deliver the soul of your living child into his kingdom. These conversations you are now having are planting seeds. There are no right words.

Soul Work

Has your child asked challenging questions? Often comfort comes through the mouths of our children. What has been your child's response?

Prayer Time

Lord, I am burdened that my child has lost a sibling and now has to watch her family grieve. Please provide me wisdom and patience as I offer explanations and answer questions. Amen.

20

Dads Hurt Too

is wife Rachel didn't realize he was grieving. A lifelong church member, Brent was shielding his wife from unwanted phone calls, planning the funeral, and just trying to be strong to keep the family together. A doting husband and father, he was busy holding his wife and letting her cry. And he was busy selling his truck, because it didn't get him to the hospital fast enough when he found that Rachel had gone into labor and soon after delivered their nineteen-week-old twin girls. Although others might not have known the extent, Brent was grieving in a big way and was torn because he couldn't fix the pain. At one point he cursed God and shouted out to him, "Am I not a good enough dad to Hunter? Was I working too much? Could I not provide enough? Did I miss church too much? How could *you* hurt me and Rachel like this?"

You see, dads can hurt too.

Have you and the father of your child had problems of late? Grief does that. It can make relationships rocky. Beloved, right now I want us to focus on accepting each other's style of grieving. God made each of us unique. Our differences also manifest in the way we grieve. There is no right way or wrong way to process loss. Repeat that statement. It is dangerous to expect our spouses to grieve the same way we do. It is also dangerous to compare the level of grief each of us feels. Unrealistic expectations will cause us much pain and set us up for disappointment and severe marital heartache.

After my miscarriages, I wanted my husband to cry those salty tears right with me. He didn't. Instead he took care of me. He made sure I ate, gave me hugs, made sure I didn't even have to think about household duties. But he quickly returned to his work. As I stepped back from the situation, I realized it was idiotic of me to think he and I would grieve in the same style. He's not one to burst into tears, but he will have an intimate conversation about issues with me. And he is a caretaker.

Loss is hard. Do not make it more difficult by fighting with the father of your child. You must realize that the two of you will not process this loss the same way.

Research the differences between men's and women's manners of grief post-loss. Men tend to experience less intense and enduring grief than women.[1] One study found that many men express grief differently than women as men tend to cry less, are less distressed when seeing other pregnant women, and have less need to talk about the loss.[2] So this means we can expect that we will cry more and we will want to verbally process our loss. Furthermore, our partners might not understand our anger when we see women who are pregnant. We need to explain to them why this hurts our souls.

Men are also confused as to how they should behave. They are not sure what is appropriate and believe that men need to deny their own feelings for their partner's sake.[3] Isn't that interesting? Many men try to guess how we want them to grieve and then follow suit. They often push their own feelings under the rug in an effort to take care of us. Most men assume we need them to be strong, so they are reluctant to share their hurt. It's rather sweet but maddening when we just really want them to cry.

Here are a few looks at different grief reactions. Hopefully this helps you realize how different every single man is when it comes to mourning.

Some of our husbands will go through a period of deep questioning, anger, and mourning.

Brent, whom we just met a few paragraphs ago, spent several years in his spiritual rebellion. He was mad at God and mad at himself, because he couldn't fix the pain. He never blamed his precious wife, but he instinctively wondered if God was punishing him. It was when his wife was going through a high-risk pregnancy with their daughter Hailee that he realized his twins have a life far better than we have on earth. He realized he had to focus on the family he has here and release his anger that was verging on depression. He says he woke up and said, "I need to realize it's my kids here who need their father." The ink tatooed upon his skin is his marker of the love he always carries for his girls. It was his way of letting it go. Twelve years later he says it is still hard. "It doesn't get any better, but you eventually get to a place where it's just okay. We don't get acceptance." He says thoughts of his twins are always present. When packing for vacation he wonders, "What would it be like packing for two more?" He did rediscover God through this process. He says, "At first it was harder being a Christian, but after you let it go it is easier if you put it in his hands and his plan."

Some of our husbands have intense pain, and we will grieve alongside one another.

Scott was an equal partner in the prolonged infertility and loss journey. He says, "Pregnancy loss is the story of two people's loss. I understand that the mother, in this horrific event, goes through more than most people understand, but the father of the lost baby goes through the very same emotions. Plus, we need to take care of our wives at the same time. We are taught to do this by being strong. Isn't that what we are told as a boy growing up? The man of the house needs to be strong. 'Big boys don't cry. You need to be strong.' So, when a family loses a baby from miscarriage, he feels he needs to shoulder the pain of the event but not show any weakness."

Scott talks about one of their losses: "The best thing of having a baby is the first time you hear and see the heartbeat. It's so surreal to think there is a little person growing inside your wife's belly. It is so beautiful. Then, around the eleventh week, Lynda started to bleed. All our dreams went crashing down around us. At the ultrasound appointment, I realized things were not good when the technician got up and really didn't say much. There was an odd silence in the room. What do you do? Hold each other, cry, just sit there? You could cut the air with a knife. The doctor came in and told us that our baby had no heartbeat, and she wanted to take Lynda to the hospital for a D&C. Your whole body is silent but your mind is yelling, *THERE IS NO WAY! What happened? Where is God? How can this happen to us?* My world was spinning out of control. But another voice started telling me, *Remember, you cannot cry. Keep in control. Your wife needs you.*

"I went with her to the hospital and remember crying together on the way there. They prepped Lynda and took her into surgery. When she came out, we had lost our baby and we were alone, just the two of us. But one of us was empty without a baby. She was a shell of who she was just the day before. What do I say? What do I do? How do I deal with this incredible pain that I'm feeling in my heart? The nurse came in to bring us a gift to in some way help us feel better. To make us understand. But, there's no understanding. The ride home was quiet, and the silence of losing our baby was heartbreaking. We named our baby Baby Hope. She was perfect in our hearts. What happens to a couple after the loss of a baby by miscarriage is hard to describe. First you have a strange separation. I mean, you are in the same home, but you don't say much. You walk through the halls empty, alone, quiet. The pain is so bad that saying nothing seems to take the place of talking about the loss. Every day you deal with the people that want to say how sorry they are or the ones that haven't heard about it and ask, 'How's the baby?' You have to go through the pain all over again. How do we start over again? How can we try again? Everyone says it takes time. Time isn't what I have at this age. But eventually our laughter did return."

Some of our husbands have pain and fear on multiple levels.

Hillary, who has no earthly children, says, "My husband and I had been trying for about a year to have a baby. Trying so hard to have a baby was emotional, so we stopped the aggressive measures. I had a miscarriage about a year later. I didn't know I was pregnant until I miscarried. The emotions of not being able to conceive were nothing compared to the loss of my baby. When I finally thought I might be ready to try to get pregnant again, my husband said he wasn't sure if he could, because he couldn't bear to see me go through the rollercoaster of trying to conceive and the possibility of loss again."

Much like Hillary's husband, some of our partners attempt to protect us from emotional pain, physical pain, or even from death. Your partner might even be trying to protect his own heart by saying he doesn't want to "try" for another baby. Beloved, if your husband watched as you faced your own death and watched your heart tear to pieces, he might be reluctant to try for another child. Please try to be patient with him as he sorts through the trauma. Wait a bit of time before revisiting the conversation. Give yourselves time to distance yourself from the loss before you both decide your future options.

Some of our husbands have no grief over the loss.

Your husband might not have any grief whatsoever at the loss. You had dreams from the advent of your pregnancy of how your child would fit into your future. However, your husband might not have had those same daydreams. So when the loss occurred, he was disconnected. This is often the case in early pregnancy loss. In general, the longer the pregnancy, the more intense the grief is for the father.[4]

Chad is an amazing father to his three girls. He and his wife are affectionate and obviously very in love with one another. However, he admitted that after the loss of one of their pregnancies, he didn't feel like he had lost a child. He took his wife to the D&C appointment and went right back to work the next day. With a background in medicine, he processed everything very matter-of-factly. His wife was internally struggling.

So how did they get through this? Did they argue and still feel bitterness? Actually they didn't. They were able to discuss their emotions without blaming one another, because they gave each other the freedom to grieve. Although he didn't feel the same emotions, Chad was emotionally available for Lacey after he realized the extent of her agony. He listened to her. He said he felt completely helpless to offer her support, but he was patient with her. He wants to tell other fathers not to "push your wife into feeling certain emotions, because if you push too much you'll push her away."

Lacey was hurt he wasn't grieving. She felt isolated, but she completely threw herself into taking care of herself, pouring out her heart at the altar, and mothering her other children. Was it easy? No. But they didn't allow their differences to be a wedge in their marriage. She says she used him as an emotional punching bag to unload her emotions, and she felt supported when he just listened.

Let me whisper some gentle advice: instead of judging our husbands for their reactions, we need to give them grace to grieve the way they feel best. We must also accept their support without pushing it away. I need to tell you something else. Some of you have partners who were not necessarily excited about the prospect of another child. His feelings of dread did not cause the death of your child. Please do not accuse him of such a thing. Know that he probably has great guilt for feeling that emotion. Give grace.

Have you asked your husband how he feels? In a heartfelt manner? And then listened? And not gotten angry? He might talk. He might not. Let him be.

Beloved, always articulate your feelings and voice your needs. Our husbands are not mind readers. Don't tell him you really don't want him to go to the next appointment with you when in all actuality you do want him there. This is not a time for guessing games. You both must speak honestly.

And just like we need time with our girlfriends, your husband might need some time with his tribe of friends. Give him space to refresh his spirit in the same way that you need to refresh your spirit.

Many of you have a partner that was emotionally unavailable before you got pregnant. And I know that you, above anyone else, crave support. I'm so sorry that you have a man that won't talk and is not there for you as a partner for life. Dear, you must rely on God fully. You might also consider going to counseling. See if you can give this pain the opportunity to bring you together instead of pushing you further apart.

And just like with other relationships, you must surrender to the truth that God is the only one who can provide comfort. Don't burden your spouse with more of a weight than he was designed to bear. God is the giver of comfort. We mourn in the hope of our Father, not in the hope of man.

And now, dear brothers and sisters, we want you to know what will happen to the believers who have died so you will not grieve like people who have no hope.

1 Thessalonians 4:13 NLT

Soul Work

Does your husband express grief differently than you do? Has it hurt that you grieve in a different manner? Mark a time in both of your schedules where you commit to talking about what happened and how you each feel. Tell him you need him to listen to you. Listen to him without judgment. Ask if he wants to write down his thoughts in this journal.

Prayer Time

Lord, please help me grieve alongside my husband.
Help us communicate through this trial.
Help us both grieve in hope. Amen.

21

Reconnecting with Your Spouse

H as your marriage been a bit on edge lately? Do you feel disconnected from yourself and your partner? This is totally normal.

But as we move further away from the point of loss, we need to invest time in our marriages. Right now I know it's all we can do to get out of bed, but eventually we must put energy into our relationships.

The first order of business is to give your husband grace. He might not deserve the grace, but that's what grace is—something we don't deserve. Pregnancy loss is an event most men don't fully understand. Remember our Hannah's husband from 1 Samuel 1? He didn't get her suffering. He continually questioned why she was so sad and why she couldn't eat. He didn't understand the yearning that couldn't be quenched. Our husbands might not understand our pain. This creates such a gap.

Creating new connections is one way we can invest in our marriages. Therefore it is wise of us to create new experiences in this time of post-loss. These experiences can unite us so we can better navigate grief and our future as a pair.

Be kind and compassionate to one another, forgiving each other, just as in Christ God forgave you.

Ephesians 4:32

Even if it feels as if you are just going through the motions, I challenge you to create new memories and fashion ways for you to emotionally unite. It is vital that we dedicate time to our spouses. Time to talk. Time to listen. Time to love and be loved. Time in mourning and times of seeking joy.

Here are some ideas:

- Go to a new restaurant or an old favorite.
- Go outside and look at the stars together. See if you can find the Big Dipper.
- What's your favorite funny movie you both enjoy? Set aside some time for popcorn and watching.
- Tell him what you need and compliment his actions: "Hey…I really appreciate you doing the dishes. It's a really big help to me right now." Thanksgiving helps cultivate a house of gratitude. Perhaps he will reciprocate.
- Send a silly or sexy text.
- Tell him what he did that comforted you most after the loss.
- Ask him how he is doing. Listen.
- Fill your home with music you both enjoy.
- Recreate your first date.
- Say, "What did I do today to make you love me more?" Listen. Then say, "You know what you did? This made me love you more today." Do this every day.
- Men are not mind readers. As I said in the last devotional, we must speak up for what we need. It's okay to tell him verbally or even in a text what you need from him. You can say something such as: "I know you are grieving. My heart hurts and right now I need you. Please hug me. Tell me you love me. Listen if I need to talk. Take me out of my element. Understand that I might not want sex. Be willing to show sadness or fear. Don't try to talk me out of my emotions but just listen. This is a hard journey and I don't want to lose us too. I love you."
- Give grace on a daily basis. Our model is Christ. Grace is giving us what we don't deserve. Think how much grace Christ gives us.
- Tell your husband if you want him to attend your doctor's appointment. None of us are married to mind readers.
- If you constantly feel rejected, then this might be a sign deeper problems are at hand. Were the problems present before the loss? Consider talking to a pastor or counselor for guidance or a Christian girlfriend with whom you can confide.

Soul Work

Does your husband respond most to physical touch, words of affirmation, quality time, receiving gifts, or acts of service? What about you? Take time to understand what you each need from one another by reading *The Five Love Languages* by Gary Chapman. The online test will also help you determine your emotional love language. This will serve you well as you try to draw closer to your spouse. Another great book is *A Wife's Secret to Happiness* by Jen Weaver.

Prayer Time

Lord, please give me the desire, the patience, and the opportunity to rekindle my relationship. I know our marriage is holy and sanctified by you. I must cultivate our marriage. Amen.

Cherishing
the Here and Now

The music of Bob Marley is echoing through my farmhouse. Something about reggae music makes me grin and puts my soul in a cheerful place. Does certain music put a dance in your step?

You see, I'm doing everything I can to remain calm, even though my mind is trying to drift off to places of worry.

Are you in a place of worry? My worry is about trying to have a baby again. I'm in that nervous two-week window of unease. Just waiting to see if a positive pink line will greet my eyes or if, once again, I'll see evidence of an empty womb. It's a rough spot, isn't it?

Either way I'll have angst. I know you understand. A positive means I'll relentlessly worry about losing my baby. A negative means I'll worry about why we've still not been able to conceive. And this whole process takes me back to nightmares of my two other miscarriages.

So I'm trying to take those Jamaican beats to heart right now. *Don't worry about a thing, 'cause every little thing gonna be all right.*

I'm drinking my freshly brewed French roast coffee. Bobbing my head to the beats of the steel drums. And filling up my soul by savoring life. You see, we can all make a conscious effort to give our burdens to the Lord.

Cast all your anxiety on him because he cares for you.
1 Peter 5:7

Have you ever tried to do that? Cast your cares on him? We hand over what we care about most—conceiving and giving life—and rely on him to bring it to us and through us.

Go ahead, try it. Tell God your worries and then stop, be still, and give those worries away. Now I want you to find something to cherish. Therapists call this method grounding. But that word doesn't sound too inviting, does it? I like to call it cherishing. Cherishing forces us to stop fixating on the negative and instead search for the positive gifts God has provided.

At times, it can be challenging for us to find blessings to count, can't it? Especially now. I know you are deep in the turmoil of pregnancy loss. It's a treacherous storm. One I've walked twice and am fearful I'll face again.

Yet, here we both are. Tethered to our reality. It's okay to be scared of this storm that billows around you. To straight up hate the storm, to cry out in anguish, and to curse the swirl for its very existence.

I get it. You want to go back to recent weeks or months. You want to change the course of the past. Oh, how I wish we could! But in our desires to bring back what we lost, we can choose to intentionally create a better now. *Now* is the only place we have to live. So we have to navigate the tempest that whirls around. We can't just hunker down in defeat. We must keep moving forward for the sake of our own hearts.

The Bible says: "Above all else, guard your heart, for everything you do flows from it" (Proverbs 4:23). The words are clear for us to look at our minds by cultivating a spirit of gratitude. If we don't control our minds, our minds will soon control us. We need to make an effort to train our minds to find good in spite of bad situations.

No one should ask you at this point to find good in the death of your loved baby. We won't understand that until we meet our heavenly Father. But what I'm encouraging you to do is to identify good in other aspects of your life.

Throughout the day, can you be still and look around and find three things to count as blessings? Make it a habit of mind. These blessings might be small—like not getting caught in traffic on the way to work. They might be insignificant—like enjoying a decadent slice of chocolate cake. Or they might be big—like looking out the window and witnessing a sunset drenched in colors.

Even right in the middle of the painful now, you can find glimmers of glory. Remember the goodness that other people displayed after the death of your baby. The hugs they gave. The very fact that you cradled a loved baby within your womb.

Mourning is a must, but at times we must refocus and identify happiness so we don't let our souls dwell in darkness. We can visit grief, but we don't need to make it a permanent home. Even though sadness overpowers your life right now, there are ways to find waves of blessings to cherish. God instructs us to "be thankful in all circumstances, for this is God's will for you who belong to Christ Jesus" (1 Thessalonians 5:18). Grief isn't something that easily passes. The storm will linger and revisit you, but you can be prepared for the days you are living. You know some moments will be a downpour and some moments will come on like a hurricane. But you can and will make it to calmer waters.

In the meantime, anchor your soul in gratitude for what God has provided. Hold tight, dear friend. In the midst of the tempest, choose to cherish. It will help ease your soul and calm your mind.

Soul Work

What are you worried about today? Go ahead and cast it on the Lord. Then look around. What do you see that makes your heart smile? Write it down.

Prayer Time

Lord, I pray that I will take time to recognize all the goodness of this earth. I pray that melancholy will not devour my ability to see beauty. Amen.

Sexual Intimacy
after a Loss

lthough many of our bodies are physically able to become intimate in the weeks following our loss, our hearts have trouble following suit. You've just gotten the wind knocked out of you, and the last thing you probably want to do is make out. Instead of a sex kitten, we might feel like clawing the eyes out of our spouse when they approach us, right? After my miscarriage, I didn't want to be touched because the thought of conceiving a baby burdened my soul with terror. Sheer terror.

This was far from the recipe for a romantic evening. And it can potentially drive a wedge in your marriage.

Are you having trouble with this topic?

Trust me. You are not the only one.

Your healthcare provider can instruct you when you are physically and emotionally advised to resume a sexual relationship. However, there are many factors you must overcome before you might feel comfortable with sexual intimacy.

Emotional Pain

Many women have difficulty with intimacy after loss. This is because many of us instinctively think: sexual intimacy > pregnancy > baby > loss again. We associate sex with past reality and future fears.

Many women report that they wanted no physical touch at all. Tears pouring from my eyes, I rejected my husband and told him to just let me make the first move. I don't think he anticipated that his flirting would end with him fetching me a Kleenex to catch my tears.

Telling him that you want to make the first move can be helpful because it takes away the guilt you have of rejecting him and his pain of being rejected. Try to set some guidelines. Tell him you really want him to hug you. Or that you want him to make a move.

Many women also say it is highly emotional the first time they become physical with their husband. Stella said, "I started crying right in the middle of sex." Holly said, "At the end of our first time, he rolled over and went to sleep, while I rolled over and sobbed."

Over time, sexual intimacy without emotional baggage will resume.

But please do not wait until the fear of being pregnant after loss passes before you resume intimacy. Dear mama, you will soon learn that a blissful pregnancy, free of fear, is practically nonexistent for women who've experienced loss. Waiting until this fear passes will only create a canyon between you and your husband. Let go of that goal, because it is quite unrealistic.

Start off small: holding hands, goodbye kisses, spicy texts. Intimacy needs a firm and fun foundation.

Physical Pain

Some women are fearful that sex might actually hurt. Express these feelings to your spouse, and don't hesitate to speak with your caregiver if you do have true concerns about physical pain as a result of a specific procedure.

Body Image

Brene Brown tells us that the number-one shame trigger for women is body-image fear.[1] After a loss, many of us have extra weight and feel like a failure. We are mad at our bodies for a very particular reason. It's hard to feel confident when we feel defeated.

Do you feel this way? Well, what makes you feel beautiful? Putting on fresh lipstick, working out, manicured nails, dancing to old-school rap, a pair of heels, an engaging debate? Embrace this side of yourself. Work on making yourself feel good to build your confidence. Fake it till you make it, sweet mama. I have a feeling, though, that your husband finds you just as attractive as ever. And know:

You are altogether beautiful, my darling;
there is no flaw in you.

Song of Solomon 4:7

Go for It

Other women find that they want to resume a sexual relationship as quickly as possible. This might be to regain emotional intimacy or to become pregnant as quickly as possible. Please be aware that you can become pregnant as soon as two weeks after having a miscarriage. Just fourteen days post-loss, your body can theoretically begin ovulating. Discuss whether you want to use birth control. If the two of you are divided, give it at least a week and revisit the topic.

Be Honest

Think about how you feel. Can you choose gentle, honest words to express your feelings and needs to your husband? It's okay to be vulnerable and say, "I don't feel pretty. Right now I just need you to hold my hand," or "I love you but I can't have sex right now. It reminds me too much of the loss. It petrifies me that we might accidentally get pregnant and then go through this all over again." Dig into honesty, so you can firmly pour the concrete for a new relationship post-loss.

One last piece of advice:

Before you start *trying* for another baby, put your focus on *enjoying* being intimate with your husband. This will help you both face your future as a united pair. The same is true if you know that you will never be pregnant again. Make an effort to reunite.

Soul Work

Has physical touch been absent from your relationship? Have you been hesitant? Intimacy is designed to keep us emotionally close to our spouse. It is a necessary part of a healthy relationship. Hold his hand. Kiss him. What do you love about him? Tell him why you love him.

Prayer Time

Lord, I pray our marriage will be one filled with passion and love. Please help my heart jump this hurdle. Amen.

Honor the Due Date:
Aloha to Heaven

Your due date will be tear-soaked. There is no way for me to tiptoe around this fact. It's the day you imagined greeting the newest addition to your family.

Once we find out we are pregnant, we often type our information into the Internet and instantly receive the day our child might enter the world. Did you do that? I did. We can find out very early when our child is due, and many of us get confirmation of that date via the growth scans on the ultrasound. Even though we know the date is only an estimate, we hold it close to our hearts.

Many of us wonder what exactly we are supposed to do on our due dates. Or on the day our child was born into heaven. Do we honor the day? Let it pass with only a thought? Create a ritual? The answer is completely up to you. You should choose how you want to spend the day. Whatever you choose is perfectly okay, and you reserve the right to sit on the couch with a pint of ice cream and binge-watch television. Give yourself grace.

One of the sweetest tales I've heard is of a lovely family who celebrates the birthday of their son Chance with a visit to his gravestone. Balloons are released, cupcakes are baked, and the sweet friends of this family send tokens of love. Brittnie and Brandon's handsome son Chance was born sleeping at five months. They cuddled with him for five precious hours. Brittnie, in a beautiful social media tribute, says to her son, "I will always love you and miss you, and I appreciate how your short life continues to point us back to what truly matters ... Jesus, shining light, and eternity. Your little life did not leave little impact. I love you, my son. I wish you were here, but I am honored to be your mommy even if we are separated for this short time. Happy birthday, baby boy!"

Her hope is in heaven, but she and her family, including her two young daughters, Clara and Camille, find comfort in celebrating Chance each and every year. Camille is firmly convinced that Chance now resides in the paradise known as Hawaii. Brittnie says, "I tried to correct her, but I guess heaven is a bit like Hawaii, right?"

One of the most inspiring tales I've heard is of a beautiful mama who spent her first due date pouring blessings on another mama/baby pair. Shalmai suddenly developed preeclampsia at seventeen weeks. Her handsome son Silas was born much too early, but she did get to hold him for a bit of time.

When the due date of her son arrived Shalmai mourned. Her eyes were swollen and her heart was heavy. She says, "I didn't know how I was supposed to spend my day today. I didn't know how I was supposed to feel or think. I braced myself for impact. After sitting on the bathroom floor (in tears) with my husband this morning it came to me. The Lord led me to the idea that I was to bless a baby boy born today."

So Shalmai prepared a basket of items for a baby boy and purchased thank you cards and goodies for the nurses who had taken care of her while she delivered her son. With a tearful trek through the hospital, she left the gifts at the nurse's station. Later she found out that the recipient was a single-mother who was financially in need. The mother left her a single yellow rose.

We might not all be led to make such a brave walk into the very hospital where we delivered, but we are all courageous.

Therefore we do not lose heart. Though outwardly we are wasting away, yet inwardly we are being renewed day by day. For our light and momentary troubles are achieving for us an eternal glory that far outweighs them all. So we fix our eyes not on what is seen, but on what is unseen, since what is seen is temporary, but what is unseen is eternal.

2 Corinthians 4:16–18

Here are some ideas for you to consider as you anticipate the bittersweet arrival of this special day. Brittnie, who is also the author of *Desert Song*,[1] says for her the days leading up to the due and birth date are more agonizing than the actual date. She says having a plan in place is best.

Please know we have enough guilt without stacking additional blocks on the pile. It is perfectly acceptable if you recognize the day by helping another, helping yourself, or doing absolutely nothing. While working through grief, we must trust our instincts. I've never actually honored my due date with more than a quiet smile, thinking of the babes I have in heaven and a prayer of thanksgiving that I will hold them one day. To me, this is a perfect ritual. We all navigate grief differently.

Ideas for Honoring Your Due Date

- Treat yourself to a pedicure, manicure, or something indulgent.
- Go on a special date with your husband or best friend.
- Have a balloon release.
- Plant a tree or flower.
- Prepare a basket for a mama/baby pair who might be in financial need and take it to your local hospital.
- Donate a pregnancy loss book such as this one to the hospital or your healthcare provider's office. Write a personal note inside.
- Prepare a basket for a mama who has just experienced pregnancy loss and take it to your local hospital.
- Take a day to do something you enjoy. My friend took the day off to spend a restful day in the mountains engaged in something she finds peaceful—photography.
- Bake cupcakes and enjoy them. Or take them to a place such as a nursing home where they can be enjoyed by members of our society who are often forgotten.

- Buy yourself a token of remembrance to wear. Laurel Box and other retailers have beautiful options.
- Donate items to a child who is now the same age as the child you have in heaven. Perhaps send an age-appropriate toy or book to a local school or church with a note asking the teacher to gift the item to a child in need.
- Bless a living child by making a donation in your child's honor to an organization that specializes in adoption and foster care, such as Bethany Christian Services.
- Help a woman facing an unplanned pregnancy by donating to a crisis-pregnancy center. This can help a mother who has chosen life.
- Find a quiet spot to pray.
- Spend the day in nature. It helps us see the bigness of the world.
- Keep yourself busy with work or activities.

Soul Work

How did you find out your due date? What is the date your baby was due? What day was your child born into heaven? Write down what you think you might want to do on your due date. The days leading up to this date are challenging. Many women report that having a plan is helpful.

Prayer Time

Lord, help me fix my eyes on what is unseen.
Help me build my faith, so it carries me on
the days where pain visits and visits. Amen.

Celebrating the Baby:
Creating Rituals

A nurse gently told Leann that it might be helpful to have a memorial for her sweet baby. Something tangible to touch and keep. So three decades ago, Leann cross-stitched a poem and included the name and date of her beloved babe: the third baby Leann had lost to miscarriage. The frame continues to be a peaceful reminder of the child she named Catherine Rose.

We all need something concrete that symbolically connects us with our child who lives in heaven. I hope you are finding this journal a place that is an ode to your loved one.

It brings our eyes peace to gaze upon a gentle reminder of the love we experienced. It's helpful to name our child, it's helpful to memorialize our child, and it can be helpful to make plans for the days we know will be challenging.

Have you already been dreading holidays? Or your due date?

What about a memorial service? Have you considered that possibility? We think of memorial services as a big ceremony. One that requires several ingredients. But they don't have to be big or elaborate. Memorial services are helpful because they are "valuable in marking time, providing a means to indicate the end of one phase and the beginning of a new one."[1] Did you have a memorial service? If you didn't, I urge you to have a private one. It can be with just you and God.

That's how I said my goodbyes. I walked through the swaying green grass and went to a small hill that overlooked our pasture. The sun was saying its adieu for the day, and I went to say adieu to my dreams for these two particular children that I had lost within months of each other. I needed to release them from my attachment and hand them over to God. It was purely symbolic, nothing fancy, but highly healing. I needed an end, so I could begin again. And this private memorial was my expression of mourning.

Some families have burials, some have urns, some tattoo a reminder on their skin, while others store it all in their minds. It's all just perfect. The way you choose. But I encourage you to have words or a ritual of parting. My friends Rachel and Brent have two sets of tiny footprints framed in their living room. It's a beautiful reminder of their girls. Their ten-year-old daughter, Hailee, told me one day that she surprised her mama last year with a cake and balloons to celebrate the birthdays of her sisters in heaven. "I don't want them to be left out," she happily told me. "They need a birthday party too!" Our children can show us amazing love and create God-breathed rituals.

Mckennah didn't know she had been pregnant with twins until she delivered her daughter. She and her midwife were both unprepared when a thirteen-week-old baby also emerged. She embraced the pain one day out in nature. She says: "Last summer I was hiking, and it was as if all of the emotions of a miscarriage had hit me. I just began crying uncontrollably. I finally began to process the significance of my miscarriage. I began to wonder what her name would have been, what she would have looked like, and what her personality would have been like. I remember looking at my daughter the next day and wondering if she felt like something was missing from her life. I still wonder if she ever feels like that. I have not yet told her about her sister but will one day when she is old enough." We all need this time to cry and to process. The chapel of our holy Creator is a perfect place to talk to him.

Holidays

Holidays can be taxing. And although Thanksgiving and Easter can be difficult, Christmas can be the worst. It is when social media swirls with images of parents with their babies. Family members ask, "When are you going to have kids?" Stockings are hung, and you know a place or two is missing. You yearn, you weep, you wish, you cry. Christmas, when joy abounds, can also be a season of sadness and melancholy.

Bind these words from Philippians upon your soul. Write them on your wrist if you must. When sadness seeks to suffocate you, meditate on this truth and put the Scripture into action.

Finally, brothers and sisters, whatever is true, whatever is noble, whatever is right, whatever is pure, whatever is lovely, whatever is admirable—if anything is excellent or praiseworthy—think about such things.

Philippians 4:8

Incorporating your loved baby into family rituals can be healing. This past Christmas I saw a poignant image on social media. My friend Joanne, who delivered her daughter Sloane at sixteen weeks, was sitting on the floor with her little boy. The two of them were crafting ornaments. She wrote that they were making one in memory of Sloane to affix to the tree. Creating gave Joanne a sense of closeness to her daughter and created an heirloom to gaze upon each year.

Doing acts of service on holidays can also be a gentle way to spend a portion of the day. Often we receive more than we give.

Natalie is a woman I admire from afar. Her beautiful Eleanor was born sleeping at forty weeks. Natalie works at Disney World, and this past Christmas she was scheduled to work. So Natalie enacted a plan. She longed to be home with her husband, her little boy, and in the presence of her daughter. But these wishes were not possible. Natalie decided to surprise an unsuspecting family with a Christmas package. She wrapped up one of her Eleanor's one-year-old dresses with a toy. She wanted to gift it to a family as a way of remembering her lovely daughter. She searched for the perfect family her entire shift. Finally, out of the two hundred thousand people at the parks, she handed the present to a family and briefly sobbed her story. And the child who received the present in honor of Eleanor—well, her name was also

Eleanor. Natalie says, "I sought to bring magic to a family, and in doing so I inadvertently found magic for myself as well."

On Easter, Thanksgiving, Christmas, and beyond, your heart will tug and feel torn. But seek to make your own magic to make the day a bit more bearable.

Mother's Day

Mother's Day can also be wistful. A few years ago, God planted the idea in my mind to begin a movement called #HonorAllMoms on Mother's Day. The intent is for places of worship to light a candle or say a prayer in honor of mothers who have babies and children in heaven and all the women who long to be mothers. This year, invite your church to participate.

Dear heart, sometimes I know you feel as if you are invisible. But did you know that President Ronald Reagan set aside the month of October as National Infant and Pregnancy Loss Month? He is credited as saying:

"When a child loses his parent, they are called an orphan. When a spouse loses her or his partner, they are called a widow or widower. When parents lose their child, there isn't a word to describe them. This month recognizes the loss so many parents experience across the United States and around the world. It is also meant to inform and provide resources for parents who have lost children due to miscarriage, ectopic pregnancy, molar pregnancy, stillbirths, birth defects, SIDS, and other causes."[2] It's nice to be recognized in this formal manner, isn't it? To have a sense of solidarity. Many women join worldwide on October 15 to remember. Bereaved mothers across the world are invited to light a candle at 7 p.m. in what founder Robyn Bear calls the Wave of Light. This can be done in the privacy of your own home or in a large gathering.

On these special days that dredge up longing and pain, we should place our rest in Jesus. On these days, we need our Savior to hold our hands. Begin the day in the Word and in prayer.

How did you whisper goodbye to your love? Did you have a funeral or memorial service? Write about the service. If you didn't have one, I encourage you to light a candle and have a private goodbye.

Lord, I pray that during times of sadness I will seek out and focus on what is true, noble, right, pure, lovely, excellent, and praiseworthy. Amen.

Staying Positive
When Trying to Conceive

aking the decision to expand your family after pregnancy loss is compounded with the fear of once again facing loss or infertility. Has this already seeped into your mind?

Most every woman I have ever met navigates the same ship after pregnancy loss: the cargo is fear. But if we desire biological children, we must take hold of that rudder and forge ahead toward the rainbow—realizing that a rainbow can take many forms.

When I am afraid, I put my trust in you.

Psalm 56:3

A *rainbow baby* is the common name for a baby born after the storm of loss. Some of us do have rainbow babies that we carried in our wombs, some have rainbow babies we carried in our hearts and adopted, and some of us find our own rainbows of joy separate from our identity as mothers.

Staying positive when trying to conceive again is rather complicated. The reason is because the path is varied for each of us. Maybe IVF is in our future. Perhaps we need to eat healthy to get our PCOS under control. We might even begin taking progesterone. At the very least we might just need to have some alone time with our husband.

Acknowledge Fear

Our first step is acknowledging that fear will be present. It mig
but it's probably not going to gallop out of our lives. Mia says, "I
miscarriage in January of last year and am now almost thirty-six w

pregnant with another baby. I have battled fear and anxiety every step of the way. I never felt like I reached a safe or comfortable point in my pregnancy. I have just had to trust in the Lord and his plan for this baby. Not easy, but, Lord willing, we will meet our son in less than a month. There is *hope* after miscarriage."

Grace, who became pregnant ten years after her first miscarriage, says that time doesn't ever erase the fear. She says she was still sick with worry every single day—grasping her belly and fighting the fear. Thankfully all was okay—she now holds her precious son.

Instead of waiting for the fear to just pass, we must focus on building a healthy body, building a healthy soul, and building a healthy marriage while we are trying to conceive.

Nurture Your Body

Our bodies were made to move. Our bodies function better when we exercise. Go outside and walk. Hit the gym. Try yoga or pilates. Do jumping jacks while you watch television. Grab a Hula-Hoop (you think I'm kidding, don't you?). Just move.

Our bodies function better when we fuel them for success. It might not be the magic fertility elixir, but the thing is, a healthy diet can't hurt. I'm talking about choosing real foods. Grill the chicken instead of frying it. Don't eat from a box. Limit your intake of sugar. Drink plenty of water and limit unhealthy beverages. Your mood will improve as your body adjusts to a diet full of vegetables and protein.

Nurture Your Soul

Our souls deserve attention. Our souls were created to worship God, in joy and in sorrow, and to be in step with him. We must do those things, so we can bear spiritual fruit. Pray throughout the day. This doesn't have to be a closed-eye, kneeling-down event. Just talk to God. While you are driving. While you are cooking dinner. While you are doing anything.

What is your favorite Bible verse related to being content? Sketch it in your memory. Say it throughout the day. Craft it into your home.

Listen to gospel, Christian, or worship music. I can't tell you how my mood began improving when I turned the dial from the pop hits to songs that reflected God. I found that throughout the day the words of the songs would enter my consciousness. In the middle of the night when I woke up with anxiety? Those songs entered my narrative. It helped me keep a godly perspective. Do I still groove to all types of music? You bet. But I try to make my primary intake music that is good for my spiritual walk. Likewise, read good books. Classics, a fiction book, or an inspiring biography that will take you away from your own mind and worries.

Trying to conceive can be agonizing. Sometimes people tell us not to worry or think about it. But we have a reminder every month that we can't ignore, don't we? Refresh your spirit during this time by pouring yourself into your body, soul, and marriage.

We must also realistically ask ourselves difficult questions. Justine Froelker, professional counselor, author, and loss mom says we must determine how far we can take the infertility and loss journey. "How far are you willing to go? How much can you spend? How many losses can you endure? These are difficult questions to consider, and we must give ourselves grace that our answers to them may easily change. However, it is unrealistic and very unhealthy to think that the only outcome for happiness to this journey is with a baby in your arms. For some of us this may not happen. We must work on active acceptance of what we cannot change and respond with love and grace to what we can. And this is determining our own happy ending."[1]

Beloved, seek joy and cultivate contentment in the day you have been given. We don't look out our window to find a rainbow each day, but we are assured that the warm majesty of the sun will greet us each morning. Embrace the here and now.

Soul Work

Have you begun trying to conceive? Are you afraid? What activities bring you peace? Bubble baths, music, or physical activity? Make sure that you incorporate this into your life.

Prayer Time

Lord, help me not be fearful of the future, but content with the present. Amen.

I'm Pregnant Again!
Choosing Joy over Fear

You probably read the title and panicked a bit. Did your heart pause? I know you might not be ready to discuss another baby. That's okay. These decisions take time.

And you might not have the choice of ever seeing a positive again. I'm sorry. Our identities are not in how many or if we can have children. Be gentle on yourself right now.

But it could be that you might be thinking about trying to create life in your womb again.

Can I tell you a secret?

My heart is aflutter. Two evenings ago, I spied two lines. That's right—on a pregnancy test. I'm filled with equal parts elation and fear. Is there even a word to describe this emotion? There needs to be. Shall we invent one? How about *happxiety*?

Yep, I'm filled with unadulterated happxiety. I'm not the only one in my house who's bursting with apprehension. When I revealed the news to my husband—a man who will enthusiastically welcome into our home as many children as we are able to have—he danced with cheer and congratulations. But his blue eyes were terrified. Bless him— he tried to hide it. It creeps into all our minds, doesn't it? The "what if."

I wish we could be filled to the brim with delight about the new life blooming in my womb. But the little thing called memory prevents us from pure elation.

I need to tell you something—inklings of apprehension can remain throughout your entire pregnancy. But it doesn't have to take up a bigger space than you or I need it to. These butterflies in your heart and stomach can ease as the weeks progress past the point of your last loss, but unrest could reside in the back of your mind. But it doesn't have to define your pregnancy, and that's the difference for you and me.

You need to know this so you are not alarmed and think you are unusual. Don't feel guilty if you don't immediately embrace this news with an overabundance of elation. Trepidation happens to us all. But we have the power to dilute this fear with tools from the Spirit: "For God has not given us a spirit of fear and timidity, but of power, love, and self-discipline" (2 Timothy 1:7 NLT).

During this pregnancy, let's choose to live by the Word and not allow fear to reign over the purity of love we can possess for the child growing in our womb. The Bible is clear on the choice we should make every day.

God has fearfully and wonderfully knit a child into my womb and your womb. It's amazing, isn't it? We should rejoice!

Rejoicing is a biblical imperative. We can't waiver between loving ourselves and our baby. We must choose to fully embrace this soul that will forever be a part of our family. We are to believe and expect that we will hold this baby in our arms. To give into fear is not honoring the life of the one we are now carrying.

This is the day the LORD has made.
We will rejoice and be glad in it.

Psalm 118:24 NLT

I know you could be trying to protect yourself by not getting too excited too soon. But will it really help to withhold loving and welcoming this baby into your life? Satan whispers in our ears that we should be afraid. That God will abandon us.

During the pregnancy after another loss, I cowered in fear. Fear can greatly impact all our lives.

I hunkered in my home and pretended my belly was not expanding.

Fear can stifle our lives until we consciously decide we are not made to live a life of excessive worry.

When your heart is full of fear, grasp your belly in your loving hands and whisper to your child, "You are wonderfully and fearfully made. You are God's loved baby. I choose to cherish you now and in the days ahead."

I don't know whether this baby in my womb and the baby in your womb will be born on earth or born straight into heaven. But either way, God is good. We can trust him with our little one and choose not to fear the outcome. We are to live in the present with the gift in our womb, not in the future of our fears.

We pray and pray that we will snuggle our rosy-cheeked little ones in our arms. And you know the good news? Statistics are on your side. Less than 5 percent of women have two miscarriages in a row.

I know it's hard. But I'm holding your hand and walking right alongside you. The blood work. The ultrasounds. Anxious visits to the bathroom. Nightmares. All these events dredge up memories, and we can't walk through them alone. We must grasp the hand that God is extending while we take this journey. First Peter 3:5–6 tells us that our duty as a holy woman is to put our hope in God. We must be like Abraham's wife Sarah and not give way to fear.

Let's praise God that we have been gifted the blessing of new life taking root in our bodies and not allow fear to steal the joy of our pregnancies.

When fear seeps into our soul, let's combat it with joy. Say, "Thank you, God, for giving me the privilege of carrying your creation another day. Please quiet my anxiety with peace."

And how to bring your husband into the news? Give him grace if he doesn't immediately show mass amounts of excitement over this pregnancy. Instead of becoming angry, show him how you are choosing joy over fear. Talk about your fears, but also talk about your plan to cultivate peace in your soul.

Choose a Scripture to pray for this new life within your womb.

Lord, a baby—that you wonderfully and fearfully made—grows in my womb. You knit this child together especially for my family. Help me to peacefully cherish each day. Regardless of whether I see him or her in the months to come or in heaven, I choose faith over fear. Thank you for creating a miracle in my body. Amen.

For This Child I Prayed:
Choosing Adoption

*E*sther is an absolute delight of a person. Although she never experienced a miscarriage, she and her husband struggled with infertility. One day she was in her middle school classroom leading a discussion about a story featuring an orphan. She casually mentioned she might one day pursue adoption.

The following day was parent conference day. Not one but three mothers who worked for the Department of Children's Services approached her. They'd heard from their children that Esther was considering adoption as a path to motherhood. Each handed her paperwork and asked her to consider adopting via foster care. Wow!

After prayer, she and her husband decided to proceed. In her prayer book, she noted their decision and began the process of praying for her future child.

Several months later, they received *the* call! A baby girl was born three weeks early and had spent her first week in the NICU. Esther and her husband were soon greeted with a little girl and took Grace home one day later. Not long after, Esther was shuffling through some papers and found Grace's discharge papers. Esther discovered that her daughter's due date was exactly forty weeks from the day that Esther had begun earnestly praying for her child.

Esther says, "There is no denying that God meant for this child to be in our home. Even though I didn't carry her in my womb, I carried that child in my heart—and in the end, it's the love that matters. Our little girl will be adopted in just a few months. It's exciting to have the fostering process over, but for the most part, we feel like she's been ours since that stormy July afternoon when we saw that little swirl of red hair peeking out of the receiving blanket."

Isn't that beautiful?

I don't know how your rainbow will emerge. You might give birth to a biological child, you might carry a child in your heart, or you might have a life full of love and know all your children are in heaven.

Your story is still being written.

Jenny is our Loved Baby sister who mourned for her children and mourned for her womb after her hysterectomy. A longing couldn't be satisfied, and she pursued adoption. She says, "Adoption has completed our family. After losing the three babies and having to have a hysterectomy after Ben was born, I wasn't able to have any more children, but my heart was always for a big family. Adoption was always a possible option. We prayed for years that if it was God's will to have more children, then he would make it happen. When Maddy was eight and Ben was six, God brought Cooper to us at four months old. I found out Wednesday evening there would be a meeting at DCS at nine on Thursday morning. At noon that Thursday, Cooper was placed with us. Two years, later he became ours forever. Adoption can be difficult, but I would go back and do it all over again. Cooper completed our family. God truly gives us the desires of our hearts."

Jesus replied, "You do not realize now what I am doing, but later you will understand."

John 13:7

There are many paths to adoption. Private versus public. International adoption or domestic. Adoption can be financially burdensome. If you want to educate yourself, I recommend you begin reading Julie Gumm's book, *You Can Adopt Without Debt: Creative Ways to Cover the Cost of Adoption*. Sources such as Bethany Christian Services and your local Department of Children's Services are also helpful.

Above all, pray. And know it is okay if adoption isn't the best path for your family.

Set time aside to pray for the little ones across the world who are seeking love and peace.

Prayer Time

Lord, I pray for all the families that are called to adopt. I pray if I am called, that the desire will grow strong in my heart, so that I know it is of your will. Amen.

Embracing
a Child-Free Life

he journey of writing this devotional has brought extraordinary women into my life—precious souls who daily teach me about seeking joy and gratitude. I can't authentically speak to the experience of embracing a child-free life. So I share the words of women who can whisper hope into your soul.

Embracing the Role of Mothering

Sweet Kayla, who has had three recurrent losses and no living children, says, "I'm not sure if God will ever bless me with an earthly child or not."

But Kayla has found redemption, purpose, and the ability to focus on the *here and now* by helping others. She spends time giving an extra hand to a mother with four children, and her job as a respite care worker means she works with children. Kayla tells us, "These things don't take the place of the children I lost, but they do help. If God is going to make me wait to enjoy my gift of children till I get to heaven, then I will find ways to enjoy and have children in my life on earth." She and her husband say that having children in their lives brings joy.

Justine tells us that she fought hard to be a mother and is one, even if not in the traditional sense of the word. She says, "Learning to thrive in a child-free, not by choice, life means we must find other ways to honor our motherhood and to parent. Every day I love harder and well because of the mother my three made me. I find, ask for, and receive the gifts of other ways to mother, whether in hobbies, serving, or loving on my friends' kids. I am a mother, and mothers mother, that simple."

Sweet dears, you are caretakers. You might not get to practice this gift on your own children, but sharing your gift of caretaking can bring joy to your soul.

Helping Others

Beloved, there is something that happens in our spirits when we go outside ourselves to help others. Volunteering, especially as an advocate for loss and infertility, has helped many women. Kayla says, "The death of my children made me a strong advocate for miscarriage and pregnancy loss. My children are my inspiration. I have up and down days, but service to others helps me tremendously. I find helping others who have gone through miscarriage or pregnancy loss extremely cathartic. This is why I love helping with our Loved Baby support group and for an organization called Mikayla's Grace. We fill memory boxes for people who have experienced infant and pregnancy loss. My husband advocates for loss in his own way. His way of bringing awareness was getting a tattoo with a cross with my son Jayden's name in the middle and the initials of the other two we lost."

Knowing Your Worth

Justine reminds us, "Our whole identity cannot be in motherhood." She says we need to ask ourselves: "Who are you? What do you love? Who do you love? What gets you excited? And, how do you take care of yourself? This journey of infertility and loss is lifetime long. Grief gets different, not better. We must find, fight for, and create our happy life."[1]

Hillary tells us to hold tight to the truth that God made each of us to be different. We must stop comparing our lives. She says, "There's something in most of us that causes us to constantly look at other women's lives (whether it's their social media highlights or their beautiful kids in their Sunday morning best) and judge them. Or want what they have. We all have our struggles. Whether you see mine or I see yours, they are there. This is especially true in our situation. I firmly believe God chooses our struggles based on the strengths, talents, and gifts he gives us. Don't compare your situation to mine or to a mother who has five living, healthy children. It doesn't help you. And you will not find the answer to all the *whys* you have. Refocus those emotions into something that will bear good and healthy fruit. Love, be generous, be helpful, be kind in the memory of the children you have lost. Give them that legacy. Don't let their legacy be sadness, anger, and misery. You wouldn't want that for them in life, don't give that to them now."

Beloved, whether you pour into others, pour into your relationship with Christ, or pour into yourself, we must remember that joy takes many forms in this life. Find your way to count joy. Do you believe that goodness can be found when your desires don't meet his will? You are strong. You can be joyful. You can rejoice.

Though the fig tree does not bud
and there are no grapes on the vines,
though the olive crop fails
and the fields produce no food,
though there are no sheep in the pen
and no cattle in the stalls,
yet I will rejoice in the LORD,
I will be joyful in God my Savior.
The Sovereign LORD is my strength;
he makes my feet like the feet of a deer,
he enables me to tread on the heights.

Habakkuk 3:17–19

Hillary says, "My biggest piece of advice is to acknowledge your feelings, but don't live in your feelings. If you let your feelings consume you, you shut out everything else. You shut out love, joy, hope, faith, and peace. This doesn't mean you can never feel anger, hurt, sadness, fear, and hopelessness. But if you live in those negative emotions, you are telling God he was wrong in creating your life. We will probably never know why our beloved children are gone. And we will probably forever yearn to hold them, to see them smile, cry, and run. If we give ourselves permission, these feelings can create compassion, empathy, kindness, understanding, and love. We can become better people through our struggles. Do we want to? No. But we can and must. For ourselves and our living family and friends."

Sweet dears. You are lovely. You are loved. You are a child of God, and your worth is not in how many or if you can have children. Although this doesn't take away pain you might possess, you need to know you are enough. Dig into contentment. Your roots can bloom right where they have been planted. Focus not on the *what if* but on the *what now*. I was told after my second miscarriage that I would never have children again. Do you know my secret for processing this startling information? I stopped looking ahead and started celebrating life for what it was. This attitude transformed my life and continues to influence my day-to-day mindset. Even though the doctor was wrong, I am grateful I went through that emotional experience, because it taught me to cultivate joy in the face of trials.

Soul Work

Answer the questions Justine recommends: Who do you love? What makes you excited? How do you take care of yourself?

Prayer Time

Lord, I don't know how you have determined my life. But for now, I realize it is a life on earth without children. Please help me not to grow discontent, but rather bear fruit and recognize my glorious worth. Amen.

A New Due Date

I sit typing and every now and then glance out the window. I'm at a glorious home with sweeping views of the mountains. The Cherokee National Forest envelops me. Friends gifted me the use of this splendor, so I can focus and finish writing. It's a lovely blessing.

Although I'm really high on a hill, the mountains around me are even higher. And I know that even if I were able to ascend to the top of the crests I see, once I arrived at that spot I would see even higher peaks waiting to be climbed.

It all reminds me of a trek my husband and our two friends took earlier in our marriage. Back when we thought we could plan our lives, we decided to take one last big trip before starting a family. We saved and saved and went to South America. Peru is where we landed. I've never felt so miniscule. The mountains are grand.

We tramped through the Amazon jungle and strolled through ancient streets, each of us taking only one backpack. We had the adventure of our lives.

But the most memorable occasion came toward the end of our trip. Overlooking the site of the Incan ruins, Machu Picchu is a sky-scraping peak. Getting to the top of the peak is arduous.

The trail? Well, it is narrow, the stone steps are steep, and the trail is often untraveled.

We traveled during rainy season, and that particular morning a flood was falling. And what happens to stone when it's wet? It gets slippery.

So there we were with rain pouring and fog rolling, climbing upward on perilous rocks. We literally couldn't see the feet in front of us. We blindly trusted our leader. One foot in front of the other.

My best friend started hyperventilating and kept wanting to turn back. "What if it's not even worth it? We probably can't even see the view for all the fog." She and her husband got in a squabble about continuing. Her husband kept encouraging her, but he couldn't carry her up that mountain or take away her fear. She had to make the decision to continue by herself. Knees quivering, she dug deep and did.

"For the gate is narrow and the way is hard that leads to life, and those who find it are few"

Matthew 7:14 ESV

Every once in a while, the clouds would part, and we would get a view of how high above the land we were and how steep the plummet would be. We'd stop and be filled with awe at our surroundings.

Have you ever had that experience? Joy and fear at the same time? Exhilaration.

Panting and legs worn from the demanding hike, we finally arrived at the top of the peak.

Absolute glory is where we had arrived.

The clouds parted and the sun glittered. It was like we could reach out and touch the golden flare, we were so close to the sky.

Down below we could see the massive Incan ruins that once were hidden and overtaken with vines. But there on top of what the Incans thought of as a holy mountain, we were walking in the clouds.

Yes! Walking in the clouds. Reaching out and touching them. And there on top of that mountain were wild flowers.

Big. Brilliant. Not the kind of wild flowers we get in the South where I live. These were wild orchids. Growing atop that holy mountain.

If there ever has been an analogy to heaven, I was standing right on it.

Dear heart, I don't know if you feel it yet, but each and every day you are growing. You started this journey in the downpour. Rain unrelenting. Every step difficult. Blind faith.

It is hard, isn't it?

And right now you are still on those slippery stone steps. Trying to climb upward. Hyperventilating at times. You are trying to bloom but fearful of falling back down. Afraid how far the topple would be.

Beloved, we are all on this journey of life. A time that God promised us would be trouble mixed with beauty. But he also promised redemption. Beauty is truth, and truth is beauty, and our truth is pure unadulterated heavenly beauty.

Lean in as I tell you, if you've accepted the love of Jesus Christ into your heart, you can rest assured that at the end of this trek you will be on top of the holiest mountain of all. Heaven.

And just as I was surprised to find those orchids, we will be surprised to find our very own offspring blooming in this majestic place.

We have a new due date! Dear mama, cast off the old date and look toward the new one.

When is your baby due? "In eternity," you shall answer.

Our lives might feel completely out of control right now, and when it does you gotta grieve. But you also must look ahead.

We are on these slippery, narrow steps, because we are climbing toward eternity. And right now it *is* dangerous and rocky, but we have a sweet promise.

Weeping may last through the night,
but joy comes with the morning.

Psalm 30:5 NLT

Grieve away. You have every right to embrace those waves of grief. But grieve in hope. Stay rooted in hope, because your little one is blooming in heaven. "Then Jesus said, 'Did I not tell you that if you believe, you will see the glory of God?'" (John 11:40).

Look at all the glory around us right now. What do you see out your window? It's absolutely magnificent, isn't it? Your heart might be despondent, but we can find beauty all around.

Just think. If *our* world is this magnificent, we can't even begin to imagine the glory of *heaven*. If orchids bloom wild atop mountains on earth, what splendor has God created for us in heaven?

Take heart. Our child is in heaven right now. We are on earth. And we must continue this trek. Find joy in the trek until you reach that holy crest.

Because in just a little while, that is where you can be. For eternity. Reconnected with your babe.

When your life starts spinning out of control, try to look ahead. Because you know what? There is nothing on this earth that is promised. Nothing we are in control of. The only thing we know for certain is that the ending of our hike is us meeting up with our baby in the presence of God. This is our new due date. And we must do everything we can to make sure those who are here on earth with us will also make that trek.

"I consider that our present sufferings are not worth comparing with the glory that will be revealed in us" (Romans 8:18).

Soul Work

Beloved, are you saved? Have you truly accepted the gift of eternal salvation? If you haven't, I invite you to pray this prayer.

Prayer Time

Father, please forgive me of my sins.
I am ready to trust you with my life. You alone
are my Savior. Your path will lead to righteousness.
I turn away from my past transgressions and
commit to having a personal relationship with you.
Thank you for loving me. Amen.

Writing Your Story

Beloved,

On the following page, you will find a place to commemorate your little love and to write your story. This might be painful, but it will serve you well to celebrate your baby in this manner.

Capture your memories. Cherish your treasure. I've left some of the spaces blank, so you can record what you want and what you know. Also paste photographs or mementos that capture your child.

Each of our losses is different. You've come alongside women throughout this book who have different experiences. Some were stories of beauty in the ashes, and some stories brimmed with pain. Don't be ashamed of your story. It's your truth, and however it happened it did.

I've prayed many prayers for you, dear reader. You are loved. And I do hope that the wildflower within comes back with magnificence.

Much love,
Sarah

Cherishing My Loved Baby

Name:

Due date:

Birth date:

Siblings:

We found out we were expecting on:

Mama's reaction:

Daddy's reaction:

Who we told:

Story of birth into heaven:

Sweet gestures made by others to tribute you:

How we have chosen to honor you and move forward:

Mementos:

Appendix

How We Mourn

The Four Tasks of Mourning model, developed by Dr. J. William Worden, shows us how many people process grief.[1] These tasks don't occur in any particular order or within a certain time frame. We all live a very different experience.

Worden uses the term *tasks*, because it shows us that we can be actively involved in the process of mourning. This helps us not feel held hostage by our grief. Knowing this framework can help you better understand what you are feeling now and in the months ahead. I've modified it a bit to speak to the specifics of pregnancy loss.

Worden's Four Tasks of Mourning

Accepting the reality of loss | Task 1

Acceptance is saying goodbye to our loved baby. Rituals such as: a funeral, a memorial service, a private burial, or even the planting of a tree are all concrete ways of saying goodbye. Have you done any of those? If not, know that the act of completing this book by journaling and commemorating your baby is a beautiful way to express your love. If your loss was early, you might not have earthly remains. I didn't. So consider choosing a piece of jewelry or creating a memory box. I especially love the mementos found at laurelbox.com. You might write a letter to your baby or release balloons. Lighting a candle and saying a special prayer is also a ritual of parting. This is a very personal decision that is up to you. There is no way that is wrong or right. But it does help to do something.

Working through the pain of grief | Task 2

This might take weeks, months, or for some, years. It is not easy for us to trod through grief, is it? It will hurt. You'll have sadness and anger. Jealousy and self-blame. Physically you might have nightmares, loss of appetite or increased appetite, loss of hair, etc. Be gentle on yourself. Invest in activities that bring you peace. Express your hurt: Write. Draw. Sing. Cry. Pray. Talk to a friend. Read the Bible.

Adjusting to life without your loved baby | Task 3

Pregnancy loss is a unique loss. Suddenly we lose our baby. We lose our identity as a pregnant woman, and we lose our hopes and dreams with our child. Some of us even lose our ability to biologically have children. In the days and months ahead, we must let go of our pregnant self and the future dreams we had for this particular baby. We have to live in our new normal and simultaneously recognize that our little one is in heaven.

Maintaining a connection to your loved baby while moving on with life | Task 4

Dear one, we can't stay swathed in our sorrow. We must choose to live. There is life all around us, and we must invest our energy into loving other people and experiences. Moving forward does not mean we are saying we never loved the child in our womb. It means we are honoring the life God has provided. We must reinvest our emotional energy to our present life.

Additional Reading

For an additional list of recommended reading and websites, please visit **allamericanmom.net**

Acknowledgments

I can no other answer make but thanks.
And thanks, and ever thanks.
—William Shakespeare, *Twelfth Night*

Dear one, I have prayed for you since this mission was first whispered into my soul. This book includes my own stories, taken from my experiences after my miscarriages and then fighting the stifling fear of being pregnant after loss. But this book would not have been possible without the brave women whose names and stories glitter on these pages. Thank you for sharing your heart treasures with me and now the world. You will help so many.

My heart bursts with love for my family. Thank you, Mom, for sharing your story and giving time to help other loss mamas with your encouraging words. Thank you, Ruthe, for being the chief babysitter (and Gary too!) and for gifting me Scripture and modeling resilience after unthinkable tragedies. I don't know how you do it. The lessons I've observed from you have helped mold these pages in extraordinary ways. Jesse and Lauren are forever loved. To Dad and my father-in-law, Dale: you both model hard work and perseverance and have gifted me the treasure of always being surrounded by nature. To my siblings by birth and marriage: Dustin, Mary, Gretchen, Michael, Cathy, and Marc I'm grateful for your prayers and big encouragement from the advent. And my grandparents, the moral compasses of my life: Faye, Granddaddy, Poppa, and Nana—for always modeling the importance of reading the Bible, prayer, and love of family.

Oh my friends! Tonya, Jonathan, Chrissi, and Jason. I'm so happy we do life together. Our passports are updated (for real this time!). Shall we try to adventure again? Leighann, Josh, and Kelly, this book wouldn't have been written had it not been for that gift of the cabin in the hills. Amber and Jason, I just adore you both. My Jill, Rachel, and Brent, you are part of this in unspeakable ways. Lacey, thank you for the laughter that brightens my soul. Joy, thank you for the heartfelt prayers, Blake for the technology assistance, and thanks to all my other beloved friends who have supported this endeavor in so many ways.

My writing champions! Dr. Thomas N. Turner and the Legion for teaching me to write and research. My kindred spirits: Bethany and Jennifer. It was love at first hello. My agent, Blythe: for saying yes after you said no and for crafting this into a beautiful love song to women. You, my dear, are amazing. For the BroadStreet Publishing team: thank you to Carlton and David for wanting to make a difference in the lives of women by breathing life into this book.

A gigantic heap of gratitude to Lynda, Kayla, Julie, Rosemary, Brittnie, Jennifer, and Cayci—you are the Loved Baby Support Team. Thank you for using your time so others do not grieve alone. Thank you to the team of advisors I've had along the way: especially Dr. Griffith and Dr. Moore. Contemporary Women's Health: thank you for checking on my heart in addition to checking on my health. If only all women were so lucky. Brother Russ and Laura Maples, I appreciate you for helping in ways you don't even realize. And to Annette, who decades ago was told after her stillbirth, "Well, sometimes you lose one." This is for you in hopes that no woman shall ever hear those words again.

And I'll end with the absolute biggest loves of my life: my Perry, Titus, Sophie, and Beckham. We shall always seek joy (shall we begin with Brer Rabbit at the Magic Kingdom?). I adore you—you are my sunshine and my double rainbow.

Notes

Chapter 1

1 Eller, 2014, 202.

Chapter 2

1 Brier, 2008; Smith et al., 2006; Wong et al., 2003.

2 Brier, 2008; The American College of Obstetricians and Gynecologists, 2015.

Chapter 5

1 The American College of Obstetricians and Gynecologists, 2015.

2 Yancey, 2013, 34.

Chapter 6

1 The American College of Obstetricians and Gynecologists, 2015.

2 The American College of Obstetricians and Gynecologists, 2016.

3 Bardos et al., 2015.

4 The American College of Obstetricians and Gynecologists, 2010.

Chapter 8

1 The Metropolitan Museum of Art, 2015.

Chapter 9

1 Worden, 2009, 196.

2 The American College of Obstetricians and Gynecologists, 2013,

3 Richards, 2014.

4 Worden, 2009, 76.

5 Worden, 2009, 77.

6 Carusillo, 2017.

Chapter 10

1 Harling, 1988.

2 Mora-Ripoll, 2010, 58.

3 Mora-Ripoll, 2010, 60.

Chapter 12

1 Bardos et al., 2015.

2 Richards, 2014.

Chapter 15

1 The American College of Obstetricians and Gynechologists, 2010, 336.

2 March of Dimes, 2014.

3   March of Dimes, 2014.

4   American Association of Pro-Life Obstetricians and Gynecologists, 2016. Chapter 16

1   The American College of Obstetricians and Gynecologists, 2015.
2   The American College of Obstetricians and Gynecologists, 2015.
3   Allen and Marks, 1993, 63.

Chapter 17

1   Lasker and Toedter, 2000, 365.

Chapter 18

1   Edwards, 2009, 213.
2   Stockett, 2009, 274.

Chapter 19

1   Allen and Marks, 1993, 240.

Chapter 20

1   Brier, 2008, 461.
2   Beutel et al, 1996, 252.
3   Puddifoot and Johnson, 1997, 837.
4   Worden, 2009, 196.

Chapter 23

1   Brown, 2015, 23.

Chapter 24

1   Blackburn, 2017.

Chapter 25

1   Brier, 2008, 462.
2   Bear and Brown, 2009.

Chapter 26

1   Justine Froekler, LPC, 2017, interview with Sarah Philpott, January 30.

Chapter 29

1   Ibid.

Appendix

1   Worden, 2009, 39–53.

Bibliography

Allen, M., & Marks, S. (1993). *Miscarriage: Women Sharing from the Heart*. New York, New York: John Wiley & Sons, Inc.

American Association of Pro-Life Obstetricians and Gynecologists. (2016). *What is AAPLOG's position on treatment of ectopic pregnancy?* Retrieved from http://aaplog.org/about-us/our-mission-statement/

Autumn L. Carusillo, P. L. (2017, February 24). When to Seek Counseling after a Pregnancy Loss (S. Philpott, Interviewer).

Bardos, J., Hercz, D., Friedenthal, J., Missmer, S., & Williams, Z. (2015). A National Survey on Public Perceptions of Miscarriage *Obstetrics and Gynecology, 125* (6), 1313–1320.

Blackburn, B. (2017). *Desert Song: Claiming Joy while Walking in the Wilderness* Bloomington, IN: WestBow Press.

Briar, N. (2008). Grief Following Miscarriage: A Comprehensive Review of the Literature. *Journal of Women's Health, 17* (3), 451-464.

Brown, B. (2015). *Rising Strong*. New York: Spiegal & Grau.

Edwards, E. (2009). *Resilience: Reflections on the Burdens of Gifts of Facing Life's Adversities*. New York, New York: Broadway Books.

Eller, S. (2014). *The Mended Heart: God's Healing for Your Broken Places*. Grand Rapids, Michigan: Revell.

Harling, R. (1988). *Steel Magnolias*. Dramatists Play Service, Inc.

March of Dimes. (2014, May). *Ectopic Pregnancy*. Retrieved from http://www.marchofdimes.org/complications/ectopic-pregnancy.aspx

Mora-Ripoli, R. (2010). The therapeutic value of laughter in medicine. *Alternative Therapies in Health and Medicine, 16* (6), 56-64.

Puddifoot, J. J. (1997). The legitamacy of grieving: The partner's experience at miscarriage. *Social Science & Medicine, 45* (837).

Richards, S. (2014). Someone I Loved Was Never Born. *Time, 184* (21/22), 60–63.

Smith, L. S., Frost, J., Levitas, R., Bradley, H., & Garcia, J. (2006). Women's experiences of three early miscarriage management options. *British Journal of General Practice*, 56, 198–205.

Stockett, K. (2009). *The Help*. New York: Amy Einhorn Books.

The American College of Obstetricians and Gynecologists. (2010). *Committee Opinion: Moderate Caffeine Consumption During Pregnancy*. Retrieved from http://www.acog.org/Resources-And-Publications/Committee-Opinions /Committee-on-Obstetric-Practice/Moderate-Caffeine-Consumption -During-Pregnancy

The American College of Obstetricians and Gynecologists. (2015). *FAQ: Early Pregnancy Loss*. Retrieved from http://www.acog.org/Patients/FAQs /Early-Pregnancy-Loss

The American College of Obstetricians and Gynecologists. (2011). *FAQ: Ectopic Pregnancy*. Retrieved from http://www.acog.org/Patients/FAQs /Ectopic-Pregnancy

The American College of Obstetricians and Gynecologists. (2016). *FAQ: Repeated Miscarriages*. Retrieved from http://www.acog.org/Patients/FAQs /Repeated-Miscarriages

The Metropolitan Museum of Art. (n.d.). *Death Becomes Her: A Century of Mourning Attire*. Retrieved from http://www.metmuseum.org/exhibitions /listings/2014/death-becomes-her

Wong, M. K., Crawford, T. J., Gask, L., & Grinyer, A. (2003). A qualitative investigation into women's experiences after a miscarriage: implications for the primary healthcare team. *British Journal of General Practice*, 53, 697–702.

Worden, W. J. (2009). *Grief Counseling and Grief Therapy: A Handbook for the Mental Health Practitioner* (4th ed.). New York: Springer Publishing Company.

Yancy, P. (2013). *The Question that Never Goes Away: Why*. Grand Rapids, Michigan: Zondervan.

About the Author

Sarah Philpott, PhD, lives on a cattle farm in Tennessee. She is the mother of three young children and wife to one hard workin' farmer (who has been her sweetheart since high school). Sarah is a former elementary teacher and went on to earn her PhD at the University of Tennessee. She is an award-winning writer who has contributed to numerous academic books such as *Contemporary Social Studies: An Essential Reader* and has been published in scholarly journals such as *Social Studies and the Young Learner*. Sarah also contributes to places such as the Huffington Post, Her View from Home, BonBon Break, Bethany Christian Services, and Pregnant Chicken.

These days, Sarah happily chooses to be a stay-at-home mom and spends her days cleaning peanut butter and jelly off the counter, dreaming of traveling the world, hosting "get-togethers" for her friends and family, and chasing her kids around the farm. She doesn't believe in sharing desserts. Life is too short to share chocolate! Sarah is a lover of big earrings, black coffee, front-porch rocking chairs, star-gazing, river days, Doris Day, and all things Hemingway. Cherishing the life God has provided is her mantra.

Sarah is also the founder of the Loved Baby pregnancy loss support group and the #HonorAllMoms Mother's Day movement. Visit with Sarah at allamericanmom.net where she writes about life on the farm and cherishing life in joy and sorrow.

allamericanmom.net